# The Truth of Terrorism

Why the Anglo-American "Great Game" of Terrorism in Afghanistan is Failing and the True Path to Global Peace

Akhtar M. Qassimyar, M.D.

iUniverse, Inc.
New York   Bloomington

The Truth of Terrorism
Why the Anglo-American "Great Game" of Terrorism in
Afghanistan is Failing and the True Path to Global Peace

iUniverse books may be ordered through booksellers or by contacting:

iUniverse
1663 Liberty Drive
Bloomington, IN 47403
www.iuniverse.com
1-800-Authors (1-800-288-4677)

Because of the dynamic nature of the Internet, any Web addresses or links
contained in this book may have changed since publication and may no longer
be valid.

ISBN: 978-1-4401-5051-7 (sc)
ISBN: 978-1-4401-5052-4 (ebk)

Printed in the United States of America

iUniverse rev. date: 7/20/2009

This book is dedicated to all people who desire to know the truth about the War on Terror and the solution to the problem of global terrorism.

# PREFACE

In this book, I share with you the truths and facts I have witnessed throughout my life in Afghanistan, Pakistan, the Kingdom of Saudi Arabia, and the United States of America. This book explains the most important global issue of our present time. It will resolve most of your questions regarding the Taliban, Al-Qaeda, Osama bin Laden, global terrorism, and how a sustainable peace is achievable in Afghanistan. It explains the specific geopolitical objectives that motivated the former Soviet Union's and the United States of America's invasions in Afghanistan. This book addresses specifically the fundamental reasons for the hostilities between the Al-Qaeda, the Arabs and the Islamic world at large on one side, and the United States, Great Britain, and Israel on the other. It covers both side of the story and clearly explains how the hostilities between the Muslim world and the Anglo-American-Israeli alliance (AAIA) be eliminated in order to make a peaceful world.

The twenty-five chapters of *The Truth of Terrorism* are summarized as follows:

Chapter 1 briefly describes the undefeated Afghan nation, the foreign invasions and some of the most important aspects of the Afghan culture. Chapter 2 explains the Afghanistan social and political situations before the Soviet Union Invasion. Chapter 3 explains the specific geopolitical objectives of the former Soviet Union for when it invaded Afghanistan in 1979.

Chapter 4 reveals the United States CIA's support of extremist Islamic parties during the decade-long Soviet-Afghan War in 1980s.

Chapter 5 describes the Northern Alliance separatists' coup of 1992, and the Era of Warlordism in Afghanistan. Northern Alliance was a coalition of warlords predominantly comprised of minorities living mostly in Northern Afghanistan.

Chapter 6 describes the United States' specific geopolitical objectives in invading Afghanistan in 2001. One of these was to secure oil transport in pipelines from the Caspian basin through Afghanistan to the Arab Sea and Indian Ocean. Caspian oil reserves are estimated to be the second largest in the world and are valued at over $11 trillion. Recently discovered natural gas reserves in the northern parts of Afghanistan are estimated to be on the order of 1.7 billion barrels.

Chapter 7 presents the unambiguous evidence that both the United States and Great Britain were involved in the foundation of the Taliban from its beginning as part of the effort to defeat the Anti-American Islamic Brotherhood parties in Afghanistan. Chapter 8 traces how, after the Taliban defeated the four anti-American radical Islamic Brotherhood parties in Afghanistan, the United States expelled its own enemy—the Anti-American Osama bin Laden—from Sudan to Afghanistan, in part to justify the invasion of Afghanistan as part of the United States' long-term, geopolitical goals in the region. In 1996, Osama bin Laden was in Sudan living in exile. The Sudanese government then expelled Osama bin Laden from Sudan to Afghanistan at the specific request of the United States. Osama bin Laden came to Jalalabad City in eastern Afghanistan in May of 1996 in a charter jet.

Chapter 9 demonstrates how Hamid Karzai was chosen by the US State Department two years prior to the 9/11 tragedy to be the next president of Afghanistan after the Taliban.

Chapter 10 traces how the United States occupied Afghanistan in a deliberate, three-step plan to implement its long-term geopolitical objectives, just as the former USSR and the British Empire had done in the past.

Chapter 11 shows the devastating social and cultural consequences and the numerous human tragedies suffered by the Afghan people as a result of the ongoing US-led war in Afghanistan. Chapter 12 is devoted to the issue of women's rights in Afghanistan, while chapter 13 discloses the facts surrounding the multi-billion dollar heroin business and its beneficiaries in Afghanistan.

Chapter 14 compares the USSR and the USA invasions in Afghanistan.

Chapter 15 describes the necessary steps for achieving a sustainable peace in Afghanistan.

Chapter 16 explains the primary reason for the hostility between the Muslim world and the AAIA. In chapter 17, the book more generally explores the reasons for animosity between the Arab world and the AAI alliance. In chapter 18, the specific reasons for animosity between the Al-Qaeda and the AAIA are described.

Chapter 19 explains the differences between Al-Qaeda and the Taliban, while chapter 20 explains why Saudi people in particular are more hostile to the USA government, despite a staunch Saudi-US alliance.

Chapter 21 reports some true stories of terrorism and provides evidence to show the real perpetrators of global terrorism.

In Chapter 22, the book explains how to end the hatred and hostility between Arabs, Al-Qaeda, and the Muslim world on one side and the AAI on the other toward making a more peaceful world. While one-quarter of the world's population may be Muslim, the key to global peace is in the hands of the AAIA, not by warfare, but by changes in policy.

Chapter 23 examines some facts about the United States' claims regarding human rights and equal opportunity.

Chapter 24 clarifies the historic fact that the British Empire occupied one quarter of the world, but never succeeded in occupying Afghanistan, while the last chapter reveals the historic fact that the priceless Koh-i-Noor Diamond in the Tower of London was in fact taken from Afghanistan during the first Anglo-Afghan war in mid–1850s. These might seem unrelated topics, but insofar as a major thread running through the history of Afghanistan since its founding has been efforts by world-powers to rob the Afghan people of their country's own national wealth—along with much else—it is well to remember this fact as a frame when thinking not only about past-Soviet and current US activities in Afghanistan but also the language used—*terrorism* in particular—to attempt to justify those activities.

# ABOUT THE AUTHOR

After graduating from the School of Medicine at Kabul University, I left Afghanistan and fled to neighboring Pakistan in late 1981. I worked in Pakistan as a doctor to help Afghan mujahideen and refugees. In addition to my job as a doctor, I was in close contact with and was well connected to many Afghan mujahideen—Afghan leaders, and numerous politicians of various parties, who were directly involved in the Soviet-Afghan War in the 1980s in Peshawar, Pakistan. Peshawar is the provincial capital of the northwest (frontier) province in Pakistan, close to the Afghan-Pakistan border where the headquarters of the Afghan resistance and Afghan mujahideen parties were based in the 1980s. It was there that they collectively conducted and coordinated the war against the Soviet Red Army in Afghanistan.

I had full knowledge of most of the Soviet-Afghan War activities, including foreigners' involvement in the bloody war against the Soviet Union in Afghanistan. After a few years, I left Pakistan for security reasons and went to Saudi Arabia. I worked as a medical doctor in multiple hospitals and health centers for eight years in the Ministry of Health. Although I was in Saudi Arabia, I was in close contact with my friends and numerous Afghan mujahideen in Pakistan, primarily in Peshawar, who were fighting for the liberation of Afghanistan.

They kept me fully informed about the Soviet-Afghan War as well as the involvement of the United States and other foreign countries as part of their strategy to support Afghan freedom fighters against the Soviets.

In the early–1990s, I came to the United States of America. I satisfied all the requirements of the Educational Commission for Foreign Medical Graduates and successfully passed the United States Medical Licensing Examination (USMLE). While living in the United States, I constantly need to keep well informed about both Afghan politics as played by Afghan politicians and foreign countries and also the truth behind those politics. Most of the facts written in this book are based on my personal knowledge; some are either present facts or Afghan history.

I believe that the military means, heavy-handed tactics, and the political rhetoric of a global war on terrorism, have failed entirely to defeat the love people have for their freedom and independence in Afghanistan and elsewhere in the world. The increasing violence both in Afghanistan and the Middle East will not be eliminated by an ongoing war against terrorism. Indeed, the conflicts will continue unless the fundamental causes of the hostility between the Islamic world, Afghanistan, the Arab world, and Al-Qaeda on one hand and the AAIA on the other are truly addressed in order to overcome the ongoing widespread violence in the world.

The global war on terrorism launched by the United States and Great Britain is an economic war that only benefits a small percentage of the super-wealthy groups, including oil corporations in both countries, while jeopardizing the safety of millions of American and British people at home and abroad. Peace and the safety of the majority of people should have priority over the interests and prosperity this tiny percentage, but currently they do not.

My book is not written against people of any ethnicity, race, religion, or political affiliation. Its main purpose is to inform people of the true facts concerning this issue. People have the right to know the truth. Everywhere, whether in the United States, Great Britain, Israel, or any other country in the world, people are people. People are different from the governments and the politicians who rule them. Most people do not share the wrong political agendas of their governments. No matter where they live, people just want to raise and educate their children and to live in peace. Unhappily, most governments keep their people unaware of the facts and truths of a situation because they cannot sell the truth to the public, in part because the truth is sometimes that the government has only the interests of a tiny minority in mind. The public is misled by their political system. For this reason, people cannot be thought of as responsible for their governments' offensive policies, so long as they are ignorant of them or are working to change them.

I have written this book to invite you to join and share with me the truth of terrorism, and to know the factual causes of the hostility between the Islamic world and the AAIA. It reveals the motives of the war on terror in Afghanistan and elsewhere in the world. If these facts and truth are not disclosed to the people, then the war on terrorism will constantly threaten global peace and endanger the safety of millions of people in the world.

I would like to mention that I used some strong words in this book. These strong words are by no means used to offend people of whatever ethnicity, race, religion, or political affiliation, but only to foster a better understanding of the issues related in this book. Such language is only used in the context of expressing opinions or beliefs held by some in the Islamic world exactly as one encounters them. I could have used very diplomatic and soft language, but such diplomatic language does not reflect the truth and facts of the book in the exactly correct way.

My hope is that this book helps people to understand the truth and facts about the ongoing wars on terrorism in Afghanistan, the global war on terrorism, and the fundamental reasons for these bloody wars so that a sustainable peace to end the misery of millions of people may finally come about. This book is dedicated to all those who want to know the truth about terrorism in Afghanistan and elsewhere in the world. At times, some sentences are repeated to re-emphasize their importance and to reinforce better understanding of the subject. At all times, I have tried to briefly and concisely explain the facts so it is easier for readers to study this book without consuming more time.

Akhtar M. Qassimyar, MD
San Diego, California, USA

# Contents

PREFACE . . . . . . . . . . . . . . . . . . . . . . . . . . . . . . . . . VII

ABOUT THE AUTHOR . . . . . . . . . . . . . . . . . . . . . . . XI

CHAPTER 1: A BRIEF DESCRIPTION OF THE
UNDEFEATED AFGHAN NATION, THE FOREIGN
INVASIONS, AND THE AFGHAN CULTURE. . . . . . . 1

CHAPTER 2: AFGHANISTAN BEFORE THE SOVIET
INVASION AND THE POLITICAL TURMOIL . . . . . . 7

CHAPTER 3: THE SOVIET UNION GEOPOLITICAL
GOALS IN AFGHANISTAN . . . . . . . . . . . . . . . . . . . . 15

CHAPTER 4: THE CIA AND THE AFGHAN
EXTREMIST PARTIES . . . . . . . . . . . . . . . . . . . . . . . 22

CHAPTER 5: THE NORTHERN ALLIANCE
SEPARATIST COUP AND THE ERA OF
WARLORDISM . . . . . . . . . . . . . . . . . . . . . . . . . . . . . 29

CHAPTER 6: THE USA GEOPOLITICAL GOALS IN
AFGHANISTAN. . . . . . . . . . . . . . . . . . . . . . . . . . . . . 36

CHAPTER 7: THE UNITED STATES AND THE
TALIBAN. . . . . . . . . . . . . . . . . . . . . . . . . . . . . . . . . . 41

CHAPTER 8:HOW THE UNITED STATES BROUGHT
OSAMA BIN LADEN TO AFGHANISTAN. . . . . . . . 49

CHAPTER 9: THE PRE-SELECTED HAMID
KARZAI. . . . . . . . . . . . . . . . . . . . . . . . . . . . . . . . . . . 55

CHAPTER 10: THE THREE-STEP PLAN . . . . . . . . . . 59

CHAPTER 11: THE UNITED STATES SUFFERED
ONE 9/11, THE AFGHAN PEOPLE HAVE SUFFERED
MULTIPLE 9/11S . . . . . . . . . . . . . . . . . . . . . . . . . . . 66

CHAPTER 12: WOMEN IN AFGHANISTAN. . . . . . . 73

CHAPTER 13: THE UNITED STATES AND THE
AFGHAN HEROIN . . . . . . . . . . . . . . . . . . . . . . . . . . . . 78

CHAPTER 14: THE COMPARISON OF THE USSR
AND THE US INVASIONS. . . . . . . . . . . . . . . . . . . . . 84

CHAPTER 15: THE VITAL STEPS TO A
SUSTAINABLE PEACE IN AFGHANISTAN. . . . . . . 88

CHAPTER 16: THE ISLAMIC WORLD AND THE
ANGLO-AMERICAN-ISRAELI ALLIES. . . . . . . . . . . 98

CHAPTER 17: THE ARAB WORLD AND THE
ANGLO-AMERICAN-ISRAELI ALLIES. . . . . . . . . . 104

CHAPTER 18: AL-QAEDA AND THE ANGLO-
AMERICAN-ISRAELI ALLIES . . . . . . . . . . . . . . . . . 108

CHAPTER 19: AL-QAEDA AND THE TALIBAN. . . 112

CHAPTER 20: WHY THE SAUDI PEOPLE ARE
MORE HOSTILE TO THE UNITED STATES
GOVERNMENT . . . . . . . . . . . . . . . . . . . . . . . . . . . . 117

CHAPTER 21: THE UNITED STATES AND
TERRORISM . . . . . . . . . . . . . . . . . . . . . . . . . . . . . . 121

CHAPTER 22: THE CLEAR PATH TO GLOBAL
PEACE. . . . . . . . . . . . . . . . . . . . . . . . . . . . . . . . . . . . 126

CHAPTER 23: THE US CLAIMS FOR HUMAN
RIGHTS AND EQUAL OPPORTUNITY . . . . . . . . . 135

THE UNIVERSAL DECLARATION OF HUMAN
RIGHTS. . . . . . . . . . . . . . . . . . . . . . . . . . . . . . . . . . . . 145

CHAPTER 24: THE BRITISH EMPIRE OCCUPIED
ONE QUARTER OF THE WORLD, BUT NEVER
SUCCEDED IN OCCUPYING AFGHANISTAN . . . 154

CHAPTER 25: THE KOH-I-NOOR DIAMOND IN
THE TOWER OF LONDON . . . . . . . . . . . . . . . . . . . 161

# CHAPTER 1:
# A BRIEF DESCRIPTION OF THE UNDEFEATED AFGHAN NATION, THE FOREIGN INVASIONS, AND THE AFGHAN CULTURE

Ahmad Shah Durrani founded Afghanistan in 1747. Ahmad Shah Durrani was ethnically a Pashtun Afghan and was the first elected ruler of the country. His rise to power came about as follows.

In 1738 Nadir Shah Afshar (the so-called Persian Napoleon) invaded Kandahar, captured Kabul, and marched to India. At the time, Ahmad Shah Durrani was an outstanding military officer in Nadir Shah Afshar's Persian army. Nadir Afshar believed that the Pashtun Afghans had superior fighting capability. In 1747, Nadir Shah Afshar was assassinated. Ahmad Shah Durrani proclaimed independence in the east of Afshar's territory, and thus founded modern Afghanistan. In 1747, the chiefs of the Durrani Pashtun tribes met near Kandahar for a *loya jirga* (a grand council) to choose their leader. After nine days of serious discussions, the leaders agreed unanimously and chose Ahmad Shah Durrani to be their new leader.

Ahmad Shah Durrani then seized Kabul and began to consolidate and enlarge his kingdom. Ahmad Shah Durrani led the Pashtun Afghans on nine campaigns into India. Ahmad Shah Durrani added Kashmir, Sind, and the Western Punjab to his domain and founded an Afghan empire that extended from eastern Persia to northern India and from the Ammu Darya to the Indian Ocean. Ahmad Shah Durrani had twenty-three sons and ruled Afghanistan for twenty-five years. He died in 1772.

Afghanistan is located in the heart of Asia, bordering the Central Asian countries of Tajikistan, Uzbekistan, and Turkmenistan in the north, the Islamic Republic of Iran in the west, Pakistan in the southeast, and the People's Republic of China in the northeast. The population of Afghanistan is roughly twenty-five million people. All the citizens of Afghanistan are called Afghans.

Ethnically, Afghanistan is a diverse country. The largest ethnic group in Afghanistan is the Pashtun Afghans, who make up over 60 percent of Afghanistan's population. Other ethnic groups include Tajiks, Hazarah, Uzbeks, Turkmen, Baluch, Nooristani, Qazalbash, and non-Muslim minorities like Sikhs, Hindus, and Jews. Afghanistan is an Islamic country.

The Pashtun Afghans have ruled Afghanistan almost continuously since its birth in 1747. Afghanistan has been ruled only for almost ten years by non-Pashtun rulers: Habibullah Kalakani, President Babral Karmal, and President Burhanudin Rabbani. All three were Tajik Afghans. Habibullah Kalakani was a self-proclaimed king of Afghanistan, and was deposed by Afghan people after only a few months.

Throughout the ages, the region today known as Afghanistan has had a very turbulent history. Afghanistan, as a major crossroads in Asia, has been invaded by many foreigners, but none have ever succeeded in occupying the land. Alexander the Great was one of the first in modern history to invade in 329–327 BC. He moved his Macedonian troops over the Hindu Kush into Afghanistan, which was composed of provinces at the time. Alexander conquered most of the Afghan provinces including Aria (in the region of Herat), Bactria (Balkh), Sattagydia (Ghazni), and Arachosia (Kandahar). But as soon as he left for India in 327 BC, his hold on the region diminished as many of the provinces revolted.

In AD 1220, the Islamic lands of Central Asia were overrun by armies of the Mongol invader Genghis Khan, who created an Empire that stretched to the Caucasus. The Mongol devastation under Genghis Khan had severe consequences for the natives of Afghanistan. It depopulated many of the major cities and caused much of the population to revert to an agrarian rural society. However, Genghis Khan failed to extinguish or even particularly hamper Islam in Central Asia. The Muslim people continued to defy the Mongol rule. By the end of the thirteenth century, Genghis Khan's descendants had become Muslims themselves. There is some historic evidence, that the Hazarah Afghans, who comprise approximately 10 percent of the Afghanistan's population, that they are in fact the direct descendants of Genghis Khan and his Mongol hordes.

During the nineteenth century, the competition between the British and Russian Empires resulted in three Anglo-Afghan wars. The British were concerned to protect colonial India from Russian invasion. Afghanistan would have been a crossroad for a Russian invasion of British India.

Shah Shuja Durrani allied himself with Great Britain and ruled as king of Afghanistan from 1803 to 1809 and then again from 1839 to 1842. Deposed in 1809, he was later restored to power in 1839 when Great Britain invaded Afghanistan in an effort to place a pro-British government back in power in Kabul.

The British invasion resulted in the first Anglo-Afghan War (1839–42), and resulted in the total rout of the British army. All sixteen thousand troops of the British Indian force were destroyed by Afghan warriors in 1842, except for Doctor Brydon, who was left to reach Jalalabad alive, probably to tell of the defeat to the British government. The pro-British king Shah Shuja was assassinated in Kabul in 1842, shortly after the British army was defeated in Afghanistan.

During the second Anglo-Afghan War (1878–80), the British were defeated in Maiwand Kandahar in 1880, and again failed to occupy Afghanistan.

The third Anglo-Afghan war occurred in 1919 when Amanullah Khan, the ethnic Pashtun King, rejected British control of his foreign policy and declared Afghanistan fully independent. In this case, the British defeat resulted in full independence for Afghanistan from the British Empire in 1919. In sum, the three British invasions from 1838 to 1919 resulted in the deaths of over twenty thousand British and Indian troops and the killing of numerous Afghan warriors.

Afghanistan remained a sovereign and independent country until the USSR invaded in 1979. On December 27, 1979, the USSR invaded Afghanistan with two specific geopolitical objectives in mind (detailed later in this book). President Hafizullah Amin was killed and Karmal's pro-Soviet regime was installed in Kabul in his place. Following this invasion, the Afghan people anticipated a long war with the Soviets. They could foresee that the USSR intended to occupy Afghanistan as it did Tajikistan, Uzbekistan, Turkmenistan, and others. The Afghans eventually defeated the USSR, and the Soviet Union completely withdrew its forces from Afghanistan on February 15, 1989. The Soviet-Afghan War started in 1979 and ended in 1989. During that almost ten-year period, it is estimated that around 1.5 million Afghan were killed.

On October 7, 2001, US and British forces simultaneously attacked Afghanistan. The Anglo-American allies toppled the Taliban government of Afghanistan, and then, on December 5, 2001, appointed Hamid Karzai at the US-sponsored Bonn conference in Germany as the next ruler of Afghanistan, though his real power at the time was extremely circumscribed. This marks simply the latest in a long line of attempts to force governments who are not pro-Afghani on the Afghan people.

Afghan history proves that the defeat of the Afghan governments by foreign invaders does not mean controlling the Afghan people. The present widespread fighting in Afghanistan between the Afghans and US-led forces is a clear indication that Afghan people are fighting for their sovereignty and independence just as they did against the British Empire and the Soviet Union.

To date, the Afghan nation is undefeated for the reason that freedom is an integral part of Afghan culture. The Afghan nation is one of the most freedom-loving nations in the world. For this reason, it is very difficult for foreign invaders to occupy the Afghans' country. During foreign invasions, fighting against invaders for liberation becomes the national past time.

Afghan people have a rich and noble culture. They risk their lives to help others. They are straightforward, honest, and cooperative people. Culturally, Afghans are peaceful people. Afghanistan was one of the safest countries in the world prior to Soviet and US invasions.

Afghan culture respects and tolerates other religions and cultures. Afghanistan is a Muslim country, but there are many non-Muslim Afghan minorities. In the twenty-five years I lived in Afghanistan, I did not hear of a single Hindu, Sikh, or Jew being killed because he or she belonged to a different religion or had a different ethnic or racial background. The Afghan culture treats people equally. Afghan culture does not accept different castes with special privileges within the Afghan society.

I fled Afghanistan at the age of twenty-five. Previously, there had been a lot of tourism in Afghanistan, especially from European countries. There was no evidence that a single tourist was killed or harmed by Afghan people throughout the country at that time. Afghans are hospitable people, and hospitality is a big part of the Afghan culture.

Afghan people try their best to resolve their problems peacefully, because retaliation is another integral part of the Afghan culture. In the Afghan culture, the intentional killing or hurting of innocent people is inexcusable. Afghan people recognize that violence and bloodshed do not resolve issues, but only increase and complicate problems. One might look at the history of Afghanistan and think otherwise, but remember: retaliation is an integral part of the culture. To resort to violence, or invasions, invites a necessary response. For this reason, the best way to resolve a problem in Afghanistan is through non-violence and peaceful means.

# CHAPTER 2:
# AFGHANISTAN BEFORE THE
# SOVIET INVASION AND THE
# POLITICAL TURMOIL

Afghanistan was a beautiful and safe country with excellent educational opportunities, free health care, and political freedom.

Afghanistan had one of the best educational systems in the region. There was free education for both boys and girls from elementary to the highest level of education.

After graduation from high school, a nationwide examination for all high school graduates throughout the country was given. All the students who successfully passed the examination were eligible to complete their higher education in universities free of charge. The students were given scholarships by the Afghan government to pay for dormitories, food, books, and all other relevant expenses. Kabul University, which was co-ed, was one of the best universities in the region.

Academically, I achieved the highest performance in the class throughout all years of high school. I completed my twelve-year academic diploma in nine years. After graduation from high school in Khoost province, I passed the nationwide examination and met the required scores for admission to medical school at Kabul University. I studied at medical school free of charge for six years. There was free housing, and breakfast, lunch, and dinner on a daily basis were also free. The food included three to five freshly prepared menus for all students, and was of good quality. The cost was entirely paid by the Afghan government. All necessary books were distributed at no cost. I was admitted to Kabul University school of medicine in 1974, and completed my medical degree in 1981.

There was coeducation at the university, and the female students had free choice in their dress. Some of them dressed according to Islamic code while others dressed in western-style clothing.

Afghanistan had a free health care system. Almost all the hospitals were free of charge. All medical doctors received salaries from the government and delivered free health services to the public in all hospitals throughout the country on a daily basis. Many doctors opened private clinics in the evening after they completed their official duty of serving the public.

There was no exception; even the highly educated and experienced professors at the school of medicine in Kabul University were delivering free health services in Ali Abad Teaching Hospital in Kabul. The Ali Abad Hospital was delivering free health care in all medical specialties, including surgeries, pediatrics, gynecology, obstetrics, eye and ENT specialties, psychiatry, orthopedics, burn and trauma specialties, internal medicine, infectious diseases, and so forth.

When I was in Afghanistan, I did not know the meaning of homelessness, for the simple reason that there were no homeless people in Afghanistan. In Afghan culture, families and close relatives were responsible for supporting the mentally or physically disabled or elderly. Afghan culture does not allow people who cannot take care of themselves to be abandoned on the streets. Afghan culture guarantees the living of disabled people so they can live in dignity and respect just as any other member of the family.

King Amanullah Khan started modern educational, economic, social, political, and judicial reforms as early as 1919 in Afghanistan, soon after he achieved full independence from the British Empire. Some of the reforms included giving equal rights for women, freedom of the press, discouraging the veiling and seclusion of women, introducing secular education (for girls as well as boys), adult education classes, and anti-smuggling and anti-corruption campaigns. Amanullah Khan was one of the most popular kings of Afghanistan and ruled from 1919 to 1928. The Afghanistan reforms started almost simultaneously with the Bolshevik Revolution of 1917 in the Soviet Union

Before the Soviet invasion, there were multiple political parties in Afghanistan: including conservatives (right) and democratic (left) of radical, secular, and religious affiliation. There were no restrictions on political activities, and any unjust act of the government was reacted to by massive, peaceful demonstrations and strikes led by the political parties in order to deter the Afghan government from any unfair acts towards the people. Afghanistan had a parliament and Senate (*Wulasie Jarga and Mushrano Jarga*). All the members were chosen in nationwide elections.

Before the Soviet invasion in 1979, there were many political parties in Afghanistan. Two parties in particular, the Khalq Democratic Party and the Parchum Democratic party, were politically the most active and succeeded in securing governmental power in Afghanistan in 1978. Both the Khalq and the Parchum parties were secular parties, and most members of these two parties were teachers, students, medical doctors, engineers, and educated people.

The political platforms of the Khalq and Parchum parties were almost the same and aimed to help the poor people of Afghanistan under the slogan of "Food, Clothing, and Shelter for all". The Khalq and Parchum parties were almost similar to the Benazir Bhutto's Pakistan's People's Party (PPP) in the neighboring Pakistan.

'Khalq' means 'people' in the Pashtu language. The members of the Khalq party were predominantly Pashtun Afghans. The leader of Khalq party was Noor Mohammad Tarakie, who was an ethnic Pashtun Afghan.

'Parchum' means 'banner' in the Farsi language. The Parchum party was smaller than the Khalq party, and its members were predominantly Tajik Afghans. The leader of the Parchum party was Babrak Karmal, who was an ethnic Tajik Afghan.

Both the Khalq and Parchum parties were pursuing similar political ideology, but the Parchum party was more pro-Soviet than the Khalq party.

Mir Akbar Khyber, one of the prominent politicians of the Parchum party, was assassinated in Kabul in 1978. The death of Mir Akbar Khyber resulted in massive peaceful demonstrations regulated by the Khalq and Parchum parties against the President Daoud Khan regime in Kabul. In response, President Daoud Khan's regime arrested almost all of the top leaders of both the Khalq and Parchum parties and put them in prison. In response to the imprisonment of the Khalq and Parchum leaders, the military officers affiliated with Khalq and Parchum parties took military action against President Daoud Khan and overthrew his regime on April 27, 1978. This drastic change is called the Saur Revolution (SR) in Afghanistan whereby the Khalq and Parchum parties seized power in Afghanistan in almost two days through military action. As a result, President Daoud Khan was killed and the Khalq and Parchum parties successfully released their leaders from jail. President Daoud Khan was a patriotic Afghan, but was a stubborn person.

After President Daoud Khan, Noor Mohammad Taraki, the leader of the Khalq party, became president of Afghanistan.

After seizing power in Kabul, the Khalq and Parchum parties made a coalition government. After a few months, the Khalq party accused the Parchum party of planning a covert military coup against the Khalq party. These accusations were not proven as politically motivated or not, but they resulted in the removal of the Parchum party from the Kabul government, leaving the Khalq party to rule Afghanistan.

Soon after the elimination of the Parchum party from power, Hafizullah Amin, the second most powerful man in the Khalq party, started an intra-party power struggle against his boss President Noor Mohammad Taraki for the top position. Amin appointed all of his loyal friends to key positions in the defense, security, and secret intelligence services in preparation for a military coup against his boss President Taraki. On September 14, 1979, Amin took control of the government by a military coup. Amin deposed and killed President Taraki, and declared himself as new president of Afghanistan.

On the day of Amin's military coup against President Taraki, I was in my brother's house in Kabul. My brother Mohammad Qassim Tanai was Director of the Central Zone and later Executive Secretary of De Afghanistan de Gatu de Satalow Adarah (AGSA), Afghanistan's secret intelligence services. That night, we had several guests in our home.

As soon as my brother came home, he called me to the backyard and told me about Amin's coup. My brother told me that tomorrow I would be killed, and that tonight was my last night of life in this world. Hearing these words, I was shocked and I asked him to tell me all the details. He told me that President Taraki had called my brother's office and asked to see him urgently. My brother continued, "Then I and the president of AGSA went to meet President Taraki. President Taraki ordered us to tell all of his supporters in the government to abort Amin's military coup against him. After that, we did what could, but it was impossible for us to abort Amin's coup against President Taraki because Hafizullah Amin and his supporters were already in complete control of Afghanistan's armed forces and the governmental key positions."

My brother continued his story and told me that tomorrow he would go to his job. Most likely, Amin's coup conspirators would try to disarm and subdue him. He told me, "I am a man of morals and principle. I will never give up, but I will respond appropriately in self-defense to Amin's conspirators." I tried hard to discourage my brother from this decision and advised him to go back to the United States of America where he had been living before the Saur Revolution. But he told me, "This is my decision what I told you. I will neither escape, nor submit to Amin's coup, but I will fight for what I believe is right. As soon as you hear the news of my death, you should leave Kabul immediately for safety reasons." After this conversation, it was nearly 2:00 AM, and we went to sleep.

In the morning, my brother said farewell to me and left for his job with the automatic gun he always carried. After several hours, I was informed that my brother and several of Amin's coup supporters were killed in a gun-battle when the coup members attempted to subdue him in his AGSA office. As soon as I heard the news of my brother's death as a result of an armed conflict that also killed several high-ranking members of Amin's coup supporters, I left Kabul immediately and went to a remote location due to the Amin's government persecution.

I was there for a few weeks. Faqir Mohammad Fakir became the new minister of the interior in President Amin's new cabinet. I knew Faqir Mohammad Fakir, and he made an indirect contact with me through one of my relatives and encouraged me to come to Kabul in order to finish my last year of medical school at Kabul University. Mr. Faqir sent me his message and said to me, "Were you a member of the Khalq party, you would have cause to be in trouble, but you are not a member of the Khalq party, so there is no reason for you to worry because the coup was entirely an intra-Party phenomena of the Khalq party." I believed what the interior minister said, and I came to Kabul.

President Hafizullah Amin ruled Afghanistan for just a few months. After killing President Noor Mohammad Taraki who was the founder of the Khalq party, President Amin felt very concerned about his own safety and moved his presidential office to the Tajbeg Palace, which was in the outskirt of Kabul.

Then, the Soviet Union invaded Afghanistan on 27 December 1979. Almost immediately, President Hafizullah Amin was killed. The Kremlin installed Babrak Karmal as the new President of Afghanistan soon after the invasion.

# CHAPTER 3:
# THE SOVIET UNION GEOPOLITICAL GOALS IN AFGHANISTAN

The installation of Babrak Karmal as the new president of Afghanistan was not only a political change. Before the Soviet invasion, Babrak Karmal had been living in exile in Moscow. He was a Tajik Afghan and the leader of the Parchum party, which was predominantly composed of Tajik Afghans. President Amin had been a Pashtun Afghan, and led the predominantly Pashtun Afghan Khalq party. Thus, the Soviet Union transferred presidential power from the majority Pashtun to the minority Tajik in Afghanistan by putting President Karmal in power.

As such, the first Tajik president in the history of Afghanistan was also the one who ruled the country from 1979 to 1986 during the Soviet Union invasion.

Leaders in the Soviet Kremlin felt they could trust the minor ethnicities to rule Afghanistan for two reasons:

The minorities of Tajik, Uzbek and Turkmen Afghans had historic relations with the Soviet Union, because Tajikistan, Uzbekistan and Turkmenistan were already part of the former USSR. By contrast, the Pashtun Afghans did not have such historic relations with the Russians.

They knew that the Tajik, Uzbek, Turkmen, and other minorities were not able by themselves to rule the majority. For that reason, the minor ethnicities would need Soviet support to rule Afghanistan, and could therefore be easily manipulated. By contrast again, the majority Pashtun Afghans did not need foreign support to rule Afghanistan.

On the night of December 27, 1979, the Soviet Red Army invaded Afghanistan. Soviet troops— including KGB and Special Forces from the Alpha and Zenith groups—dressed in Afghan uniforms and occupied major governmental, military, and media buildings in Kabul. The Soviet operation began at around 8:00 PM in Kabul.

On that specific night, I was in a restaurant with a couple of my friends having a dinner. While dinner was being served, the restaurant manager told us to leave for safety reasons because there were widespread gunfire and artillery sounds in Kabul. We left the restaurant. On the way to the Kabul University's dormitory, I witnessed the Tajbeg Presidential Palace of President Hafizullah Amin under fire and heavy bombardment. The Soviet troops destroyed Kabul's communications hub, paralyzing the Afghan military command.

To justify the invasion of Afghanistan, Moscow said it wanted to help the new Karmal regime to defeat Islamic extremists, Arabs, and foreign fighters, as well as Anglo-American imperialism and other reactionary forces in Afghanistan toward establishing a democratic government in the country. In fact, the USSR invaded Afghanistan in 1979 for two geopolitical objectives.

> To incorporate Afghanistan into the USSR, just as Tajikistan, Uzbekistan, Turkmenistan, and other countries had already been, and

> To expand the Soviet Union's borders to the south to reach through Pakistan to the Indian Ocean and to the oil rich countries in the Persian Gulf region.

During the Soviet invasion of Afghanistan in 1979, the United States and its Western allies panicked at the idea of tens of thousands of Soviet troops in Afghanistan in close proximity to the oil-rich regions of the Persian Gulf and Arab peninsula. President Jimmy Carter insisted that such Soviet aggression could not be viewed as an isolated event of limited geographical importance, but had to be contested as a potential threat to US influence in the Persian Gulf region.

After the Soviets invasion, Pakistan's military president General Zia-ul-Haq supported and heavily armed the anti-Soviet Afghan resistance. Pakistan's government supported the Afghan mujahideen resistance largely to keep the Soviet-Afghan War inside Afghanistan, because Pakistan was the next target if the USSR was going to continue to expand its borders to reach the Indian Ocean and Persian Gulf region. Afghan mujahideen refer to those freedom fighters who were directly involved in fighting against the Soviet Army for the liberation of Afghanistan.

For the reasons to protect their own interests, both the United States and Pakistan were the greater supporters of the Afghan mujahideen who were fighting against the USSR in the 1980s. In all, there were seven Afghan mujahideen resistance parties headquartered in Peshawar, Pakistan that were coordinating and conducting military operations against the Soviet army in Afghanistan. In addition, the United Kingdom, and Saudi Arabia were major financial contributors to the Afghan mujahideen resistance.

After the election of President Ronald Reagan in the United States, aid for the Afghan mujahideen significantly increased in 1981. The United States was helping Afghan mujahideen by $600 million per year. One of the most important weapons supplied by the United States to Afghan mujahideen was the FIM-92 Stinger anti-aircraft missile used for shooting down the Soviet and Soviet-allied Afghan warplanes.

The United States and UK were encouraging Saudi Arabia, Egypt, Kuwait, and other Arab allies in the Middle East to send Arab fighters to wage jihad (or "holy war") against the Soviet Union in Afghanistan. One of the notable Arab fighters from the Kingdom of Saudi Arabia was Osama bin Laden.

In March 1985, the US government adopted National Security Decision Directive (NSDD) 166, which established a number of military tactics for the Afghan mujahideen to use against the Soviet Union and the Soviet-backed Afghan government in Afghanistan.

Under the direct instructions from the CIA Director William Casey, the CIA initiated programs for training Afghans in techniques such as car bombs, assassination, and in cross-border raids inside the USSR.

In order to defeat the soviet Union, the CIA placed greater pressure on the mujahideen to commit terrorist operations in Afghanistan, like damaging power lines, knocking out radio stations, blowing up government office buildings, hotels, cinemas, attacking both civilian and military targets, knocking out bridges, closing major roads, attacking convoys, disrupting the electric power system, attacking police stations, assassination of government officials, ambush of government employees, shooting at vehicles, laying mines in government accommodation or houses, using poison, and so on. Many Afghan mujahideen rejected and did not agree to use these kinds of military tactics in Afghanistan because such military operations were considered by many Afghan mujahideen as un-Islamic. However, some other mujahideen justified these kinds of military tactics against the Soviets and used these military tactics and strategies during the Soviet-Afghan War in Afghanistan. As a result, the mujahideen supported by United States and its allies carried out over six hundred terrorist acts a year in Afghanistan from 1982 through 1987.

For example, in March 1982, a bomb exploded at the Ministry of Education, damaging several buildings. In the same month, the Naghlu power station near Kabul was blown up and darkened the city. On September 4, 1985, a domestic Bakhtar Airlines plane was shot down as it took off from Kandahar airport, killing all fifty-two Afghan civilians aboard. One of the victims was Dr. Nazar Muhammad, who was my best friend while we were students in Kabul University.

The United States and its allies were involved either directly or indirectly in all of these terrorist war tactics and strategies.

The long-term Soviet-Afghan War was very expensive for the USSR. The Soviet Union was spending approximately £2.5 billion sterling per year in Afghanistan, which was a considerable drain on the USSR's economy at that time. Eventually, the General Secretary of the Soviet Communist Party Mikhail Gorbachev said that the main reason that there had been no national consolidation to date was because Comrade Karmal was hoping to continue sitting in Kabul with the Russian's help.

Soon after Gorbachev voiced his dissatisfaction, the USSR replaced President Karmal with Dr. Najibullah in November 1986. Although President Najibullah adopted a new constitution and undertook a new policy of national reconciliation, the Afghan people's war for the liberation of their country was unaffected.

After almost ten years of war, the Afghan people defeated the Soviet army and on February 15, 1989, the last Soviet troops departed from Afghanistan. The country was liberated.

Since World War II, the Soviet-Afghan War showed itself to be one of the most destructive in terms of human casualties. Over the ten-year period, it is estimated that approximately 1.5 million Afghans were killed. Five million Afghans fled to Pakistan and Iran. And another two million were displaced within the country. In the 1980s, one out of two refugees in the world was an Afghan. These numbers do not begin to describe the damage to the Afghan infrastructure, especially where health and education are concerned.

After the Soviet-Afghan War ended in 1989, the Soviet Union published figures for the loss of life and materials in Afghanistan. The Soviet disclosed that they lost 14,410 army soldiers and 568 KGB employees, along with 115 aircrafts, 330 helicopters, 140 tanks, 430 artillery guns and mortars, 1,120 radio sets and command vehicles, 500 engineering vehicles, and 11,360 trucks and petrol tankers. From December 25,

1979 to February 15, 1989, a total of 620,000 soldiers served and fought in Afghanistan; 53,700 were wounded, 415,900 fell sick, and 10,755 were left permanently disabled.

# CHAPTER 4:
# THE CIA AND THE AFGHAN EXTREMIST PARTIES

During the Soviet Union invasion of Afghanistan in 1979, millions of Afghan people participated in jihad (holy war) and fought for the liberation of Afghanistan against the USSR.

In 1981, I fled to Pakistan. There were seven official Afghan mujahideen parties, headquartered in Peshawar, Pakistan, coordinating military attacks on the Soviet army in Afghanistan. Peshawar is the provincial capital of Northwest (Frontier) province of Pakistan close to the Afghan border.

Mujahideen refers to those freedom fighters who were directly involved in fighting against the Soviet forces for the independence of Afghanistan.

The seven Afghan mujahideen parties were essentially divided into extremist Islamic parties and moderate Islamic parties. Four of the seven Afghan mujahideen parties were classified as extremist parties, the so-called Islamic Brotherhood parties, which included:

Hekmatyar's Hezb-e Islamie party

Rabbani-Masoud's Jamiat-e Islamie party
Sayaf's Itehad-e Islamie party
Khalis's Hezb-e Islamie party

These four parties basically had the same ideology and political platform. They were originally a single party in Afghanistan called Ikhwan-ul Muslimeen (Muslim Brothers) but later split. These four radical Islamic parties were not only fighting for the liberation of Afghanistan, but also were struggling to make an Islamic government ruled by Islamic law (Shariah) once the Soviet army was defeated and had withdrawn.

Three of the seven Afghan mujahideen parties were moderate, and included:

Mojadidie's Jabha-e Mili Nijat party.
Pir Gailani's Mahaz-e Milie party.
Mullah Mohammadi's Harakat-e Inqilabie-e Islamie party.

Generally, in all Muslim countries in the world, radical Islamic parties—including the four radical Islamic parties in Afghanistan—have anti-American, anti-Israeli, and anti-British ideology. The radical Islamic parties are very specific and clear in their hostility towards the United States of America, the state of Israel, and the British government. The radical Islamic parties believe that Israel occupied the Holy Mosque of Al-Aqsa in East Jerusalem in 1967, with the military and political support of the United States of America and the British government.

All Muslims, which comprise one quarter of the world's population, are unhappy with the occupation of Al-Aqsa Holy Mosque whether they are radical or moderate Muslims, and whether they are Sunni or Shiite Muslims. The only difference between the radical and moderate Muslims concerning the Al-Aqsa Holy Mosque issue is that the radical Islamic parties are specifically struggling to liberate the Al-Aqsa Mosque from any non-Islamic force that would occupy it, which are currently Israel with the backing of the United States. However, the moderate and the mainstream Muslims are not involved in direct confrontation against the United States and the Israeli government, but are simply unhappy and angry at the occupation of the mosque and consider the Al-Aqsa occupation as a disrespectful US-Israeli policy in regard to the Islamic world.

Al-Aqsa Mosque is the third holiest mosque in Islam after the Al-Haram in Mecca and The Prophet's Mosque in Medina, Saudi Arabia. The liberation of the Al-Aqsa Mosque in Jerusalem is one of the main goals of the radical Islamic parties in the Islamic world. For this reason, the United States makes itself an enemy of Islam by militarily and financially assisting the state of Israel in its continuous occupation of the Al-Aqsa Mosque in Jerusalem. It seems that few people in the United States are aware of, or understand, this surprisingly basic point. Perhaps even the US government sometimes loses sight of how it offensive it must be—for a country that promises freedom of religion—to give vast sums of aid to support numerous Israeli governments that have sought to prevent Islamic religious expression. And while it must be almost impossible to imagine that radical Islam could vanish overnight with the de-occupation of the Al-Aqsa Mosque, nevertheless such an event would destroy an enormous part of the appeal of extremist Islam.

The United States viewed the Soviet invasion of Afghanistan in 1979 as an integral Cold War moment and a direct threat to the United States' interests in the oil-rich countries in the Arab peninsula. In 1979, the United States authorized funding for Afghan guerrillas and started armament of Afghanistan's mujahideen as part of the US Central Intelligence Agency (CIA) Program Operation Cyclone (POC). During the Soviet-Afghan War (1979-1989), the United States was one of the major financial and military contributors to the Afghan mujahideen. Numerous weapons, including the FIM-92 Stinger anti-aircraft missile systems, were donated to Afghan mujahideen and were very effective in shooting down the Soviet aircraft during the war.

While I was living in Peshawar, Pakistan, I noted how the United States government and the CIA were more supportive of the extremist Islamic parties of the Afghan mujahideen than they were of the moderate parties.

One night, I visited Professor Hakim Taniwal in his home in Peshawar, Pakistan. Professor Taniwal was a professor of sociology at Kabul University and a member of Pir Gailani's Mahaz-e Milie party, which was one of the moderate Afghan mujahideen parties. (Professor Taniwal went on to become governor of Paktia province in the US-installed government of President Hamid Karzai until September 10, 2006, when an extremist Islamic suicide bomber assassinated him in Gardez, the capital of Paktia province in Afghanistan.) Mr. Taniwal was a friend of mine and a very hospitable person. The night I went to meet him, however, he was very distressed. He told me he'd had a meeting with some CIA officials in Peshawar, who were involved in assisting the Afghan mujahideen. Mr. Taniwal asked the CIA officials for weapons for his moderate group, but the CIA rejected his request, stating they would never give weapons to his group unless Gulboddin Hekmatyar (one of the four extremist leaders) agreed to the request as well. This was because, according to the statements of the CIA officials, Hekmatyar was considered the most trustworthy jihad leader against the Soviet Union. Consequently, he and his radical party received most of the military and financial aid from the US government and the CIA during the Soviet-Afghan War.

Mr. Taniwal was distraught that night and told me that the US government and CIA support of extremist Islamic parties in Afghanistan would be extremely dangerous for peace and stability in the future even after the Soviet's defeat and withdrawal.

Currently, Mr. Gulboddin Hekmatyar and his Hezb-e Islamie party are fighting against US forces following their invasion of Afghanistan in 2001. Mr. Gulboddin Hekmatyar is now on the United States' list of terrorists because he is fighting for the withdrawal of US forces from Afghanistan.

The US government and the CIA were more supportive of the extremist Islamic parties than the moderate Islamic parties during the Soviet-Afghan War, despite the fact that the United States government and the CIA had full knowledge that the radical Islamic parties were both anti-US and anti-Israel parties.

I have been interested in Afghanistan's political and social system since 1974, when I was a student at Kabul University. I have considerable knowledge about all of Afghanistan's political parties including conservative, liberal, radical, secular and religious parties, and have familiarity with their political platforms. I know many members and politicians affiliated with different political parties in Afghanistan.

When I was in Peshawar, Pakistan in 1981, I was one of the outspoken critics of Mr. Gulboddin Hekmatyar and the radical Islamic parties in Pakistan. I was in opposition to these parties because radical Islamic parties had persecuted and killed numerous educated Afghans in Pakistan who had liberal political views or held a non-extremist Islamic ideology. All four of the radical parties were involved in the killing and persecution of educated Afghans in Pakistan, but Hekmatyar's Hezb-e Islamie and Rabbani-Masoud's Jamiat-e Islamie parties in particular murdered more scholars, politicians, medical doctors, and engineers in Pakistan than any other radical party.

In 1983, I left Pakistan and went to Saudi Arabia because I was informed that I was #17 on the hit list of one of the radical Islamic parties in Peshawar, Pakistan. I found employment in the Ministry of Health and worked as a medical doctor in the Kingdom of Saudi Arabia for eight years. When I was in Saudi Arabia, I stayed in contact with many Afghan mujahideen, politicians, and refugees who were living in Pakistan. I visited Pakistan once a year for one and a half months during my annual vacation, with extraordinary caution, to see my family and relatives.

Despite killing and persecuting numerous educated Afghans and having a radical, anti-US and anti-Israel ideology, Mr. Gulboddin Hekmatyar and his extremist Hezb-e Islamie party were considered heroes by the United States government and the CIA during the Soviet-Afghan War. This was solely because Hekmatyar and his party were fighting against the Soviet Union, a bitter enemy of the United States at the time. But now, this same hero and his Hezb-e Islamie party are called terrorists due to their effort to drive US forces from Afghanistan.

I state again that I have opposed myself to extremist Islamic parties and their behavior. Nevertheless, it is clear that Mr. Gulboddin Hekmatyar and his party are doing the exact same thing now in trying to drive foreign invaders from Afghanistan as they did in the 1980s with the Soviet Union. The difference I want to emphasize is the change of label. Those heroes, the holy warriors involved in a justifiable, legitimate and holy war against the Soviets, are now called terrorists, insurgents, involved in unjustifiable, illegitimate guerilla attacks in Afghanistan? Quite literally, only the name has changed.

Naturally, the United States' definition of terrorism is based on its own interests in the world. Hence, the US government may elect to accuse and label as terrorists any government, political organization, or individual who opposes its policies, even when those governments, organizations, or individuals are simply defending their rights against the United States occupation, aggression, and offense. The accusation of terrorism itself becomes a political tool to warn people, governments and political organizations not to attempt to defend their rights against the US occupation, aggression, or offense in the first place.

The Universal Declaration of Human Rights guarantees that all nations have the right to defend their independence and sovereignty against foreign invasions. Afghan people have the right, whether they are radical or moderate Muslims, to defend their independence and sovereignty against foreign invasions from any country, whether that is the Soviets in the 1980s or the United States at the present time, in order to liberate Afghanistan and get full independence. Based on this Universal Declaration, then, the Afghan people who seek independence and sovereignty from US aggression are not terrorists and can neither be called such nor treated as such.

# CHAPTER 5:
# THE NORTHERN ALLIANCE SEPARATIST COUP AND THE ERA OF WARLORDISM

Afghanistan is a diverse country composed of many ethnicities. Diversity is the beauty of a nation. The major ethnicity in Afghanistan is Pashtun Afghan, who comprise more than all the other ethnicities combined. Pashtun Afghans comprise over 60 percent of Afghanistan's population. Pashtun Afghans speak Pashtu language.

The other bigger ethnicities of Afghanistan are:

Tajik Afghans: Tajik Afghans make around 18 percent of Afghanistan's population. Tajik Afghans speak Farsi. Approximately one-third of Tajik Afghans are by heritage Pashtun Afghans but speak Farsi. Such Tajik Afghans are called 'language Tajiks' because they are the descendants of Pashtun Afghans but grew up in predominantly Tajik areas. The majority of the children whose parents are both Pashtun and Tajik Afghans by marriage speak Farsi. Farsi is much easier to learn than Pashtu language.

Hazarah Afghans: Hazarah Afghans speak Farsi and comprise approximately 8–10 percent of Afghanistan's populations. Hazarah are Shiite Muslims.

Uzbek and Turkmen Afghans: Uzbek and Turkmen Afghans comprise approximately 7–8 percent of Afghanistan's population. Uzbek and Turkmen Afghans speak Uzbekie and Turkmenie languages.

Tajik, Uzbek, and Turkmen Afghans predominantly live in Northern Afghanistan close to the Tajikistan, Uzbekistan, and Turkmenistan borders.

The Northern Alliance was the coalition of the warlords of the Tajik, Uzbek, Turkmen, and Hazarah ethnicities in Afghanistan who ruled the country from 1992 to 1996 during the so-called the Era of Warlordism.

Although the Northern Alliance consisted of different ethnicities, it pursued an anti-Pashtun agenda and has been struggling to make an independent country in Northern Afghanistan. The Northern Alliance was in fact a coalition of separatists. The leader of the Northern Alliance was Commander Ahmad Shah Masoud. The Alliance had two specific goals:

As separatists, they struggled to split Afghanistan to make a separate country in Northern Afghanistan.

They used anti-Pashtun rhetoric to further their cause

Of the seven Afghan mujahideen resistance parties headquartered in Peshawar, Pakistan during the Soviet invasion, six of the seven parties were predominantly Pashtun Afghans, while Rabbani-Masoud's radical Jamiat-e Islamie party was predominantly Tajik Afghans.

Commander Ahmad Shah Masoud was one of the most popular mujahideen commanders from the Jamiat-e Islamie party during the first few years of the Soviet invasion. He had strong resistance bases in Panjshir Valley, north of Kabul. Commander Masoud continued to conduct successful military operations against the Soviet army until 1983.

In 1983, however, he signed a secrete truce with the Soviet Union. From that time forward, he not only collaborated with the Soviets but also pursued a separatist (*sitemie*) ideology with a goal to splitting Afghanistan. Later, he openly became the leader of the separatist movement of the Northern Alliance.

When the Soviet-backed Najibullah regime began to crumble in 1992, the Northern Alliance separatists arranged a coup to seize power in Kabul, which would then allow them to split Afghanistan.

In fact, the separatist coalition was composed mainly of three groups. Two of these groups were part of the pro-Soviet government in Kabul, while one was part of the Afghan mujahideen resistance. The three main factions of the Northern Alliance were:

> Babrak Karmal's predominantly Tajik Afghan group within Kabul's then-ruling Parchum party of the Soviet-backed regime.

> The Uzbek, or Gilam-Jaman, militia. The Gilam-Jaman militia was a pro-Russia militia established by the Soviet Union to fight during the Soviet invasion

against Afghan mujahideen in Afghanistan. The militia was predominantly Uzbek Afghans. Gilam-Jaman means 'robbers' because the militia was infamous for brutality and stealing.

The Rabbani-Masoud's predominantly Tajik Afghan Jamiat-e Islamie party. Both the party leader Mr. Burhanudeen Rabbani and his top commander Ahmad Shah Masoud were Tajik Afghans.

On April 17, 1992, pro-Soviet factions in the government (Karmal's and the Uzbek militia) invited Commander Ahmad Shah Masoud from Panjshir Valley to Kabul and handed over the government to him ostensibly to show that the Afghan mujahideen had finally taken control. During the coup, only the President of Afghanistan Dr. Najibullah had to be removed from power, and he took refuge in the United Nation compound in Kabul. This political maneuver was dubbed the Northern Alliance separatists coup.

As soon as the Northern Alliance warlords took over Kabul, however, they proved incompetent rulers. Afghanistan quickly fell into chaos and anarchy.

Many Afghan mujahideen commanders were unhappy with the results of the coup, and started fighting against the fledgling government in Kabul. Heavy fighting erupted in Kabul.

From 1992 to 1996, more than 100,000 Afghan civilians were killed throughout Afghanistan, with approximately 60,000 civilians in Kabul alone. The city fragmented into many parts, each of which was ruled by different warlords and their armed groups. Because there was no effective government, the fragmentation in Kabul spread to the entire country, and many warlords came to rule different areas of the country.

These warlords and their armed groups were involved in looting and stealing of national banks, museums, and other national properties. The anarchy and chaos of this period in Afghanistan is called the Era of Warlordism.

The warlords and their armed groups were involved in numerous despicable crimes. In one familiar and well-documented story, a Northern Alliance commander and twenty soldiers broke into the Kabul apartment of a thirteen-year-old girl named Nahida Hassan. They killed her twelve-year-old brother and then shot her grandfather, father, and older brother. In order to avoid being raped, Nahida jumped from the sixth-floor window to her death. Today, there is a shrine where her body landed. The shrine is one of the unforgettable memorials to the grief that Afghan women suffered during the Era of Warlordism in Afghanistan. This is also but one of many such despicable crimes during the period. It should be remembered as well that Afghanistan's now-current president, Hamid Karzai, was the deputy foreign minister of the Rabbani-Masoud government during the Era of Warlordism.

During this period, Ahmad Shah Masoud was the leader of the Northern Alliance separatists and still sought to split Afghanistan to make a separate country in the north. The Alliance proclaimed Northern Afghanistan to be "Khurasan Country." Signs were placed in Northern Afghanistan that read "Welcome to Khurasan country."

At the beginning of the Soviet Union invasion, Ahmad Shah Masoud was one of the top commanders and was widely respected among Afghan mujahideen. Masoud did a great job in fighting against the Soviet army in the Panjshir valley to the north of Kabul but then betrayed the Afghan resistance and signed a secret truce with the Soviet Union in 1983.

That truce Masoud to stop anti-Soviet attacks and to keep the Salang Highway open for Soviet ground logistic transportation to Kabul. The Salang Highway was the only highway for ground transportations between the USSR and Kabul. Masoud received approximately one hundred thousand dollars per month for his collaboration. Monthly checks arrived in Kabul regularly and were endorsed by the president of the Afghanistan Bank. The money was then given to Masoud in the Panjshir Valley. I personally confirmed this information with the now-retired president of the Afghanistan Bank, who currently lives in California in the United States.

Commander Ahmad Shah Masoud's followers assert that Masoud is a national hero. In fact, Masoud was neither a national nor a Tajik hero. Not only was he involved in treason by collaborating with the enemy during the Soviet invasion, there are also many patriotic Tajik Afghans who reject Masoud's separatist ideology.

Masoud was also an anti-Pashtun commander and fought against Pashtun Afghans in the country. In practice, there was little difference between Hezb-e Islamie and Jamiat-e Islamie parties in Afghanistan. Both were just two branches of the Ikhwan-ul Muslimeen (or Islamic Brotherhood) party. Both were radical Muslim parties that had the same ideology and platforms. The only difference between Hezb-e Islamie and Jamiat-e Islamie was their ethnic background: former were predominantly Pashtun Afghans, while the latter were predominantly Tajik Afghans. In the course of his actions as a commander for Jamiat-e Islamie, Masoud regularly fought against the members of the predominantly Pashtun Afghan Hezb-e Islamie.

The Taliban defeated the Northern Alliance government in 1996, thus ending the Era of Warlordism in Afghanistan. The

Taliban defeated almost all of the warlords and their armed groups, and either left them hiding in caves in Afghanistan or saw them escaping to Tajikistan, Uzbekistan, Turkmenistan, Pakistan, and Iran. Overthrowing the Rabbani-Masoud government in 1996, the Taliban restored security and re-united the divided Afghanistan.

Afghanistan has noble culture. Afghan people have been living peacefully in the spirit of brotherhood as one Afghan nation for centuries. There are strong marital, social, and political relations between the different ethnicities in Afghanistan. Although the Northern Alliance separatists tried to split Afghanistan, they failed both because the separatists were small in numbers and because the majority of Tajik, Uzbek, Turkmen and Hazarah Afghans did not support the Northern Alliance separatists' agenda.

# CHAPTER 6:
# THE USA GEOPOLITICAL
# GOALS IN AFGHANISTAN

The United States invaded Afghanistan in 2001 to achieve geopolitical objectives just as Great Britain and the Soviet Union had in the past. These objectives were three-fold.

> To secure the southern route of an oil pipeline from the Caspian Sea through Afghanistan to the Indian Ocean.
>
> To use the Afghans' country for military and bases for secret intelligence in the region.
>
> To increase involvement in opium production. (This third goal is based on the fact that the opium production simultaneously increased as soon as the US invaded Afghanistan. Afghanistan presently supplies over 90 percent of the world heroin.)

Each of these objectives is addressed in more detail below.

## The Southern Pipeline and the War on Terror

The United States is the world's largest oil consumer and importer. After the collapse of the Soviet Union in 1991, the United States and its allies began an intense search for petroleum resources in the region. It was discovered that the world's second largest oil reserves are in Turkmenistan and the surrounding regions of the Caspian basin north of Afghanistan. Afghanistan is the bridge between Turkmenistan and Pakistan's Indian Ocean ports.

It was estimated that increasing amounts of oil and natural gas would be imported from Central Asia within the next few decades. The world's richest oil resource is the Caspian basin, which includes parts of Russia, Iran, and the five independent republics of Turkmenistan, Tajikistan, Uzbekistan, Kyrgyzstan, and Kazakhstan. It was estimated that the amount of oil in the Caspian basin was around 120–250 billion barrels, worth in excess of eleven trillion dollars. The Central Asian region north of Afghanistan is estimated to contain as much as 45 percent of the world's gas reserves.[1]

One of the long-term US geopolitical goals in invading Afghanistan was a trans-Afghan pipeline route from the Arabian Sea to the Caspian Sea basin. From an energy standpoint, Afghanistan is critically important for its geographical position as a potential transit route for oil and natural gas exports from Central Asia and Caspian basin to the Arabian Sea. This potential included the probable construction of oil and natural gas export pipelines through Afghanistan. The export pipeline was under serious consideration in the mid-1990s.

---

1    This information, and much of what immediately follows, is readily available at Wikipedia's entry for the Caspian Sea (http://en.wikipedia.org/wiki/Caspian_Seal)

In 1998, Dick Cheney commented that, "I can't think of a time when we've had a region emerge as suddenly to become as strategically significant as the Caspian." Dick Cheney was the vice president of the United States and one of the most powerful people in Bush administration when the United States invaded Afghanistan in 2001.

It was recently discovered that Afghanistan itself has as much as 1.8 billion barrels of natural gas, mostly in the Afghan-Tajik basin. In the 1970s, the Soviets estimated Afghanistan's known natural gas reserves to be approximately 5 trillion cubic feet. Afghanistan used to import about 75–92% of its natural gas output to the Soviet Union through Uzbekistan in the late 1970s.

In January 1998, the Taliban signed an agreement that would allow a proposed 880-mile, $2 billion, 1.8-billion-cubic-feet-per-day natural gas pipeline project with the Unocal Oil Company in the United States. This proposed pipeline would have transported natural gas from Turkmenistan to the Afghan border and then through the Western provinces of Kandahar and Herat in Afghanistan to Pakistan and the Arabian Sea. The news of the agreement between the Taliban and Unocal Oil Company was reported by the Afghan media.

Already, however, the United States had a plan to invade Afghanistan to secure the southern route of an oil pipeline from the Caspian Sea through Afghanistan to the Arabian Sea. The United States government was unable to sell this to the American people in its blunt and true form. Instead, the later Bush administration tried to keep the American people ignorant of the United States' long-term geopolitical goal of invading Afghanistan because the expected human losses and the financial expenses of the war were expected to be high.

The United States government was well aware of the historic fact that the Afghan people were undefeated and would resist an American invasion just as they had the Soviets in 1980s. After 9/11, however, the Bush administration successfully misrepresented the justification of an invasion in Afghanistan as part of a "War on Terror".

*Afghanistan as a Secret Intelligence Site*

Strategically, Afghanistan's geopolitical location makes it critically important for the United States as a superpower. The United States invaded Afghanistan to use the country for military and secret intelligence purposes for gathering information from countries in the area, and especially Iran and China. China is the emerging global military and economic superpower in the region.

The Islamic Republic of Iran is considered one of the most anti-American and anti-Israeli governments in the world. Presently, the United States has established an intelligence base in Herat province close to the Iranian-Afghan border in western Afghanistan for conducting covert operations inside the Islamic Republic of Iran. Afghanistan also can serve as a base of intelligence operations now or in the future into China, Russia, Pakistan, and so forth. Additionally, as part of the War on Terror, Afghanistan may be an ideal location for transporting and interrogating prisoners in that "war". The aggression also serves, potentially, to eliminate the "embarrassment" to the United States of those former allies of its in Afghanistan who are now called terrorists because they are seeking to liberate their country from yet another foreign aggressor.

*The Opium Trade*

The Taliban's Islamic government, which ruled Afghanistan from 1996 to 2001, did an excellent job of eradicating the cultivation of opium poppies in areas of Afghanistan that they controlled on the religious ground that Islam religion prohibits the use of all narcotics and drugs, including alcohol.

The United States toppled the Taliban government and occupied Afghanistan in 2001. Since the invasion of Afghanistan by the United States in 2001, the production of opium has increased exponentially in the country. Currently Afghanistan has reached the top of the list in heroin-producing and heroin-trafficking countries in the world. In the past eight years since the US invasion, drug production and drug trafficking has reached to almost sixty billion dollars annually. Based on current statistics, in the summer of 2006, the poppy harvest in Afghanistan was estimated to be 6,100 metric tons of opium.

It is unclear to what extent the United States directly benefits from such proximity to the opium industry, but vast sums of money are changing hands and heroin usage in the United States is once again reaching epidemic levels in the United States.

# CHAPTER 7:
# THE UNITED STATES AND
# THE TALIBAN

The mullahs and the Taliban were collectively a traditional non-radical Islamic class in Afghanistan. Taliban means 'religious students.' Traditionally in Afghanistan the mullahs and the Taliban lead prayers in mosques, attend funeral ceremonies, preach to people, and resolve disputes between people in the communities. During the Soviet-Afghan War the mullahs and the Taliban were not radical in Afghanistan. Contrary to the radical Islamic Brotherhood parties in Afghanistan, the mullahs and Taliban were moderate Muslims. During the Soviet-Afghan War in the 1980s, the mullahs and the Taliban became predominantly affiliated with Mullah Mohammadi's Harakat-e Inqilabie-e Islamie party, which was considered a moderate Islamic party among the seven Afghan mujahideen resistance parties.

In 1992, after the pro-Soviet Najibullah government collapsed and during the heavy fighting in Kabul between the rival radical Islamic Brotherhood parties of Hezb-e Islamie and Jamiat-e Islamie, the mullahs and the Taliban defended themselves, but were not involved in the fighting for power during the Era of Warlordism. After the defeat of the Soviet Union in

Afghanistan, the mullahs and the Taliban put down their arms and returned to their traditional Islamic clergy duties in mosques as before.

I personally know General Shahnawaz Tanai, who was the defense minister of Afghanistan from 1988 to 1990. General Tanai is not only one of Afghanistan's most experienced military generals, but also one of the most popular politicians. His last name Tanai is affiliated with the Tanie tribe which is one of the biggest tribes in Khoost province. The Tanie tribe consists of tens of thousands of people.

General Shahnawaz Tanai was Defense Minister of Afghanistan during the Najibullah government. President Najibullah was leader of the Parchum party after the Kremlin removed Babrak Karmal from power in Afghanistan. Shahnawaz Tanai was a very popular defense minister, but did not belong to the ruling Parchum party. General Tanai was member of the rival Khalq party. In 1990, the Parchum party accomplished a military coup against General Tanai to remove him from power. General Tanai fled to Pakistan and has been living in that country since then. I have been in frequent contact with him since that time.

During the Taliban government, I traveled from the United States to Pakistan and met with General Tanai in Islamabad. We had dinner one night in a restaurant in Islamabad. During the dinner, I had asked General Shahnawaz Tanai to tell me about the foundation of the Taliban in Afghanistan who were ruling the Kabul government at that time. General Tanai firmly stated to me, "It is just a political a game." I again asked him to explain to me in complete detail. General Tanai told me that before the foundation of the Taliban movement, he'd had a meeting with three Western diplomats in Islamabad, Pakistan.

One of the diplomats was from Great Britain, and the other two were from the United States.

General Tanai stated that the diplomats invited him for dinner and asked him for a specific consultation during the meeting. The diplomats stated during the meeting that the United States had defeated the Communism in Afghanistan through Islamic extremism, and now had a plan to defeat the Islamic extremism by traditional Islam in Afghanistan. The diplomats then asked for his thoughts and advice about such a plan. General Tanai told me he responded, "Although the Islamic class of mullahs are not extremist Muslims in Afghanistan, they could change to extremists in the future because they are a religious class. So, there are risks involved in this plan. In the worst-case scenario, it would be a big headache for both the United States and Afghanistan if the traditional mullahs became radical. For this reason it would be better for the United States to defeat the Islamic extremist parties by a national, democratic, and liberal movement in Afghanistan, because the democratic movement would not turn to extremism and there would be no risk involved. The best way to defeat the extremist parties in Afghanistan is through democratic, liberal, and national forces in Afghanistan."

General Tanai told me the diplomats did not agree with his advice and intended to continue with their plan to eliminate extremist Islamic parties in Afghanistan with traditional Islamic mullahs and clergy, who were not radical at that time in Afghanistan.

General Tanai told that the Taliban movement was established only a few months after his conversation with the diplomats.

In response, I told him, "You gave the best advice to the diplomats. It was safe and in the best interest of the Afghan people. I wish the diplomats had accepted it, but if they did not, that was not your fault".

Based on this conversation, there is an implication that the Taliban was founded basically by the United States in order to defeat specifically the four anti-American extremist Islamic Brotherhood parties in Afghanistan. So both the United States and Great Britain were involved in the foundation of the Taliban movement from day one in Afghanistan.

The relations between the Taliban and the United States and its allies were friendly from the very beginning.

The Taliban captured Kandahar on November 5, 1994. The United States diplomats met with the Taliban leaders in Kandahar on April 19, 1996.

The traditional Taliban movement defeated the warlords and the anti-American radical Islamic brotherhood parties in southern, eastern, and western Afghanistan.

The Taliban overthrew the Rabbani-Masoud's government of the Northern Alliance, and effectively took control of Kabul in September 1996. The traditional Islamic Taliban became an executive power for the first time in Afghanistan's history and ruled the Kabul government for almost five years. The Taliban Delegation visited US in February 1997.

Hamid Karzai, now the United State's most-trusted man, was one of the strongest supporters of the Taliban Movement (See Hamid Karzai's biography.). Later, after the Taliban captured Kabul and the United States' plan for invading of Afghanistan had ripened, Hamid Karzai distanced himself from the Taliban movement.

In July 1995, one of the United States' allies, the Saudi deputy intelligence chief, visited Afghanistan on a peace mission to meet with the Taliban government. The United States' closest ally in the Middle East, King Fahd of Saudi Arabia, stated on September 4, 1997, that the Saudi government would assist the Taliban.

The United States allies Pakistan, Saudi Arabia, and the United Arab Emirates (UAE) assisted and funded the Taliban in Afghanistan. The countries of Pakistan, Saudi Arabia, and UAE had diplomatic relation with the Taliban government.

The traditional Taliban movement defeated and considerably damaged the four anti-American Islamic Brotherhood parties. By September 2000, the Taliban had captured Taloqan, and had control of almost 95 percent of Afghanistan. In five years, the Taliban conquered almost the entire country of Afghanistan and collected weapons from the warlords and their armed groups. The Taliban had helped the United States and defeated the anti-American extremist parties in the country. The Taliban restored security and safety in Afghanistan, and reunited the divided country. The Taliban had made the once-chaotic Afghanistan ready for foreign investment. But once the United States achieved its intended goal by way of the Taliban in Afghanistan, the United States government betrayed the Taliban.

After the Taliban captured Kabul, they implemented primitive Islamic rules, because they did not have enough education about Islam. Islam reflects a huge religious knowledge and philosophy. In Islamic universities, there are many kinds of advanced degrees in different branches of Islam given to Islamic scholars. The Taliban were not Islamic scholars; in fact, most of them were young students with poor Islamic knowledge who set out to implement primitive Islamic rules in Afghanistan.

The Taliban were called the angel of peace for their outstanding achievement in restoration of peace and security in Afghanistan. But after United States' plan for invading of Afghanistan began to ripen, the political media of the US government put out considerable anti-Taliban and anti-Islamic propaganda and made a great deal about the Taliban's primitive religious rules. The US government's widespread propaganda was designed politically not only to pave way for the future invasion of Afghanistan, but also to damage the image of Islamic religion based on the Taliban primitive rulings.

In addition to having an unfortunately primitive idea of Islamic law, it must also be remembered that during the Taliban's rule, the Afghan government requested aid from the United Nations, the United States, and other allies to help open schools in Afghanistan, but the request was not granted. No aid was given to help the Afghan people to open schools in the Taliban controlled area. The Taliban were asking help for the reason that they were engaged in heavy fighting against the radical Islamic parties and the Northern Alliance warlords in Afghanistan. The Taliban were unable to pay for even basic social services, because the Taliban did not have money to pay the expenses of both war and social services simultaneously. In addition to war expenses, the United States and its allies imposed severe economic and political sanctions on the Taliban government in Afghanistan.

There was no doubt that the hardliner Taliban were unreasonably enforcing primitive rules in odd with Islamic principles, because they had poor knowledge regarding Islam. For instance, growing a beard is a good thing in Islam and many Muslim religious people—like people in other religions—

frequently grow their beards, but it is optional in Islam, not mandatory. The Taliban incorrectly implemented an optional choice as mandatory, and enforced all men in Afghanistan to grow their beards, because they believed it was a good thing.

The second example of the Taliban's unreasonable rule was restriction on music. Generally, religious Muslims believe that a good Muslim should spend more time doing good deeds in life and help people to be rewarded by God rather than listening to music. But hearing music is absolutely not prohibited in Islam. The Taliban were unreasonably imposing anti-music rules and banned music in their controlled areas.

Both growing a beard and listening to music are optional and personal matters in Islam. Islam neither enforces Muslims to grow beards nor prohibits Muslims from listening to music. The Taliban had poor Islamic knowledge, and made optional and personal matters mandatory rules. Worse still, Islam respects education and is a pro-knowledge religion, so the Taliban's prohibition of education to girls is virtually anti-Islamic. So also the violence and disrespect shown to women. These mistakes should not be excused, even when we understand how the young generation of Taliban males came to think as they did. But this mistake provides no pretext for the United States' invasion, especially when it was complicit placing the Taliban in power to begin with, and when its motivations for invading have nothing to do with the well being of the people whose country is being attacked.

The United States of America toppled the Taliban government in 2001.

In the past eight years, there have been tens of thousands of soldiers from the United States and its allies with the most advanced military weapons and technology trying to impose their will on Afghanistan from afar, without success. Because of this, Afghanistan is currently one of the most unsafe and unsecured countries of the world. By contrast, the Taliban restored security to almost 95% of Afghanistan within five years. It is especially disheartening that the current situation in Afghanistan should be a product of the Anglo-American aggression and their political blunder.

# CHAPTER 8:
# HOW THE UNITED STATES BROUGHT OSAMA BIN LADEN TO AFGHANISTAN

When I was in Pakistan in early 1980s, there were multiple Muslim volunteers from Arab and other Muslim countries coming to Pakistan in order to help the Afghan resistance against the Soviet invasion. Those Muslim volunteers were fighting against the former Soviet Union together with Afghan mujahideen in Afghanistan.

The US government was one of the major supporters of the Afghan mujahideen, who were fighting against the Soviet army. The US government was working with Saudi Arabia and Pakistan to set up Islamic schools and military training centers in Pakistan for Afghan mujahideen.

In mid-1980s, Osama bin Laden, as an Arab volunteer from Saudi Arabia, had moved to Pakistan to help the Afghan mujahideen. He established an organization called Maktab al-Khidimat (MAK) to recruit Muslim volunteers from around the world. In the 1980s, the MAK maintained recruiting offices even in the United States in Detroit and Brooklyn.

Osama's father, Mohammad Awad bin Laden, was a wealthy businessman with close ties to the Saudi royal family. Osama was born in Saudi Arabia. Osama Bin Laden is a civil engineer, and graduated from King Abdulaziz University in the Kingdom of Saudi Arabia.

When the Soviet Union was defeated and the Russians pulled out from Afghanistan in 1989, the foreign Muslim volunteers returned back to their home countries as heroes who had brought down and defeated the strong superpower of the Soviet Union.

As soon as Osama returned victoriously from Afghanistan to Saudi Arabia in 1989, he was unhappy with the US troop's presence in his own country of Saudi Arabia. The US troops in Saudi Arabia supported the royal family to rule the oil-rich Kingdom of Saudi Arabia.

Osama started anti-American struggles in Saudi Arabia in order to prompt the withdrawal of US military forces from his own country. He started frank criticisms of the ruling Saudi royal family, and was expelled from Saudi Arabia in 1991 because of those activities. Osama went to Somalia and then eventually to Sudan in exile.

In Sudan in 1992, bin Laden established a new base for military operations in Khartoum, the capital of Sudan. He continued to struggle against the US military presence in Saudi Arabia and was regularly critical of Fahd bin Abdulaziz, the King of Saudi Arabia.

On March 5, 1994, King Fahd of Saudi Arabia sent a representative to Sudan and demanded Osama bin Laden's passport. The Saudi royal family revoked Osama's citizenship and stripped him of his own Saudi nationality. Osama was living in Sudan without nationality.

In February 1996, the Sudanese government had a meeting with Saudi government to expel bin Laden from Sudan to his own country of Saudi Arabia. The Saudis refused the Sudanese government's offer and did not allow Osama return to Saudi Arabia. The Saudi government reasoned that bin Laden was born in Saudi Arabia, but his citizenship had been revoked, and he was no longer from Saudi Arabia anymore.

According to the Sudan Defense Minister Fatih Erwa's statement, the Sudanese government then offered to hand bin Laden over to the United States in 1996. The United States declined the offer. There is a clear reference even in the *9/11 Commission Report* regarding the Sudanese defense minister's statement, although the report claims it could find no substantiation for Erwa's offer[2].

The United States turned down the Sudanese government offer in 1996 to expel Osama to the USA, despite the fact that Osama Bin Laden had already been involved in multiple deadly attacks on the United States[3]. Instead, the United States continued to put pressure on Sudan to expel bin Laden to Afghanistan. Finally, in May 1996, Osama bin Laden was expelled from Sudan, and sent to Jalalabad on a chartered jet.

---

2       See   http://en.wikipedia.org/wiki/
Osama_bin_laden for instance.

3       See   http://articles.latimes.com/2001/
dec/05/opinion/oe-ijaz05

On August 7, 1998, a pair of truck bombs exploded outside the US embassies in Kenya and Tanzania killing more than two hundred people. Osama Bin Laden was allegedly blamed by the United States for the explosions.

Nearly two weeks later, on August 20, 1998, President Bill Clinton ordered cruise missile attacks against Sudan and Afghanistan. The United States cruise-missile attacks killed twenty Sudanese citizens and destroyed the Al-Shifa pharmaceutical plant in Khartoum, which used to produce most of the affordable medicine in Sudan.

After the cruise missile attacks on Sudan and Afghanistan, the Sudanese government sent a high-ranking government official to the United Nations in New York. The Sudanese official was very frustrated and unveiled interesting information to the UN about how Osama Bin Laden was expelled from Sudan to Afghanistan. The Sudanese government official clearly disclosed how Osama had been living in exile in Sudan from 1992 to 1996. The CIA then requested the Sudan government to expel Osama from Sudan. The Sudan government accepted the United States government's request and had asked Osama to leave Sudan. Osama accepted.

The CIA also asked the Sudanese government to inform them about where Osama was going. The Sudanese government asked Osama where he had planned to go from Sudan, and he said either Somalia or Afghanistan. The CIA specifically requested that bin Laden not be allowed to go to Somalia or any other country, but that he should be expelled to Afghanistan instead. The Sudanese government thus sent Osama bin Laden by chartered jet from Sudan to Afghanistan based on the United States' specific directive.

During the US cruise-missile attack on Sudan and Afghanistan on August 20, 1998, I was curious to know the official Sudanese government's statements in the United Nation about Osama bin Laden. I was persistently following the news and media. The Sudanese official did not disclose detailed information on whether the CIA had asked them to expel Osama to Afghanistan via a false passport—false, because his passport had already been revoked by the Saudi government in 1994—on who provided Osama's passport to travel to Afghanistan in the first place, or whether Osama was expelled from Sudan to Afghanistan without any passport or other legal travel documents at all.

The Sudanese official proclaimed that the Sudan government did whatever the CIA had asked for. The Sudan government had accepted the US's request to expel Osama bin Laden from Sudan and agreed with it. Despite this cooperation with the United States, the US still attacked Sudan with dozens of Tomahawk cruise missiles, killed civilians, and destroyed the most productive pharmaceutical factory in Sudan.

Similarly, after the United States cruise-missile attacks on Afghanistan on August 20, 1998, the Taliban government foreign ministry emphasized how both the United States and Osama had helped the Afghan people during the Soviet-Afghan War in 1980s. They noted that Afghanistan did not have any issue with Osama; however, if the US government wanted to capture Osama in Afghanistan, the Taliban would cooperate. The United States refused the Taliban's offer to capture Osama in Afghanistan. This is hard to understand when not considered as an early strategic move toward setting up a reason to invade Afghanistan.

There were 192 countries in the world in 1996, but the US government specifically requested the Sudanese government to expel Osama to Afghanistan.

# CHAPTER 9:
# THE PRE-SELECTED HAMID KARZAI

I came to the United States in the early–1990s. I planned to work in my field as a medical doctor in the United States. After passing the United States Medical Licensing Examination (USMLE), I was in Providence Hospital in Washington D.C. for medical training, which was helpful in getting medical residency in the United States.

During that time, I had an accidental meeting with Ambassador Michele J. Sison in Washington DC in late 1999. At that time Ms. Sison was Deputy Ambassador of the United States in Islamabad, Pakistan.

In 1999, the Taliban were ruling the Kabul government. During the meeting, Ms. Sison asked me, "Who do you think will be the next president of Afghanistan after the removal of the Taliban government?"

I answered that the Afghan people have higher political understandings and are familiar with politics because there have been many political parties with different political platforms in Afghanistan in the past several decades. In addition to that,

Afghanistan was at war with the Soviet Union for almost ten years. However, my best answer to her question was that there were numerous popular politicians who would do a good job as president in serving the people of Afghanistan but that the United States doesn't like those politicians because they are patriotic and prefer to serve the Afghan people, rather than serving the interests of foreigners.

Then the Ambassador asked me specifically, "What would you think about Mr. Hamid Karzai to be the next president of Afghanistan after the Taliban government?"

When Ms. Sison mentioned Hamid Karzai's name to be the next President of Afghanistan, I immediately had a greater interest on the subject because one of Hamid Karzai's brothers was my classmate in Kabul University, and I was familiar with this specific last name. I told the US diplomat that Hamid Karzai would never be able to rule the country because he is not only an unpopular person in Afghanistan, but also that rulers appointed by foreigners have failed to rule Afghanistan, simply because the Afghan people don't trust them. I told her I believed Mr. Karzai would never be able to rule Afghanistan competently and he would fail.

Then the US Ambassador informed me, rather with an attitude, "The next president of Afghanistan will be Hamid Karzai."

I asked Ms. Sison if she was sure about Karzai's selection by the United States as the next president of Afghanistan after the Taliban. Ms. Sison, who was a white, skinny, and a tall lady, drew herself up and said, "I am the Deputy Ambassador of the United States of America in Islamabad and I know for sure that Karzai is the only one who will be the next president of Afghanistan."

Almost two years after that particular encounter, the September 11 tragedy happened in 2001, committed by Arab hijackers, predominantly from Saudi Arabia and approximately 3,000 people were killed in the United States.

Less than a month after 9/11, on October 7, 2001, the US attacked Afghanistan and justified the invasion as part of the "War on Terror". The US toppled the Taliban government in Afghanistan.

On December 5, 2001, the United States sponsored a conference in Bonn, Germany to appoint the head of the Interim Transitional Administration after the collapse of the Taliban government in Afghanistan. In the US-sponsored Bonn conference in Germany, the United States appointed Hamid Karzai to be the head of the Interim Transitional Administration in Afghanistan.

On June 13, 2002, a symbolic *loya jirga* (grand council) in Kabul appointed Karzai as president of the Afghanistan Transitional Administration. On December 7, 2004, Karzai was again elected as president of the US-occupied Afghanistan.

According to ambassador Michele J. Sison's statements in 1999, Mr. Hamid Karzai was chosen by the US State Department to be the next president of Afghanistan two years before the 9/11 tragedy.

According to the United States' pre-plan, Mr. Hamid Karzai became the next president of Afghanistan after the Taliban government. The US government claims about free elections, the Bonn Conference and *loya jirga* (grand council) were political rhetoric. Mr. Hamid Karzai was chosen by the US State Department in 1999 to be the next president of

Afghanistan. The unpopular Mr. Karzai was neither elected by the Afghan people nor would have been the choice of the twenty-five million Afghans.

Hamid Karzai's relationship with the United States has a long history and started during the Soviet-Afghan War in 1980s. At that time, Hamid Karzai was the top person among the Afghan mujahideen who had been in close contact with the CIA, which was involved in supporting and arming the Afghan mujahideen against the Soviets Union invasion in Afghanistan.[4]

---

4    See Hamid Karzai's biography.

# CHAPTER 10:
# THE THREE-STEP PLAN

The US invasion of Afghanistan in 2001 was preceded by a three-step plan:

First, the United States and Great Britain founded the Taliban Islamic movement in order to defeat the anti-American Islamic Brotherhood parties in Afghanistan, which were well armed. The Taliban defeated the anti-American Islamic Brotherhood parties in Afghanistan and collected their weapons, including the remaining US-built Stinger anti-aircraft missiles, which were given by the United States to Afghan mujahideen during the Soviet-Afghan War in the 1980s. The Stinger missiles were collected by the United States as a precaution measure not to be used by the Afghan mujahideen against US aircraft during the future invasion of Afghanistan. In 1996, the Taliban captured Kabul.

Second, the CIA expelled the anti-American Osama bin Laden from Sudan to Afghanistan in 1996 to provide a pretext for an invasion of Afghanistan. In other words, Osama bin Laden was sent to Afghanistan for the reason that if the anti-American

Osama attacked any US interests while based in Afghanistan, which was expected to be very likely, then the US could invade Afghanistan under the pretext of retaliation.

Third, the United States appointed Hamid Karzai as president of Afghanistan. Hamid Karzai was Washington DC's most trusted man, and was pre-chosen in 1999 by the United States government to be the next president of Afghanistan and to provide a pro-US government in Kabul.

It may seem an overstatement to see this as all carefully thought-out in advance, but even if the founding of the Taliban (by the United States or not) and the expulsion of Osama bin Laden to Afghanistan (as a future plausible pretext for invasion or not) are simply quirks of history, the selection of Hamid Karzai two years before the 2001 invasion cannot be dismissed as coincidental. Even so, the naked political aggression of starting a war with a nation that had given the US no cause to do so checked the greed of the tiny percentage that wanted Afghanistan's resources and strategic location. The 9/11 tragedy changed that, and the Bush administration used it as an excuse to invade Afghanistan under the guise of a War on Terror.

Let me be clear. There is no question that 9/11 was a tragedy for all people who live in the United States. As an Afghan myself, I understand the value of retaliation. But the US government did not go to Afghanistan solely—perhaps not even primarily—in retaliation. They went for the sake of a preexisting desire to gain access to energy resources and militarily strategic locations. In brief, they did not go on the American people behalf, but for the sake of a tiny percentage of US citizens.

The US and British invasion of Afghanistan was not the only one in recent history to be conducted based on false accusations under the banner of the War on Terror, since it was followed by the invasion of oil-rich Iraq in 2003. The US and the UK promulgated a tremendous amount of propaganda against Saddam Hussein's government in Iraq and repeatedly accused Iraq of having weapons of mass destruction (WMD) in 2003. Links between Hussein an Al-Qaeda were also fabricated, and both of these lies have been exposed as such since. Nevertheless, the United States and Great Britain went on to oust Saddam and place someone favorably disposed to them in power.

The US government used corruption and mega-bribery to assist the invasion of Afghanistan. Just prior to it, the CIA of the Bush administration doled out approximately seventy (70) million dollars to the ousted Northern Alliance warlords in Afghanistan to win their support in order to collaborate with the United States in invading Afghanistan. This sum of money was divided between the different Northern Alliance warlords, who now are currently part of the present ruling government in Kabul. I personally know one of the warlords in Afghanistan who received approximately one million dollars.

After the invasion, the United States restored the ousted Northern Alliance warlords to power to rule the country at a Bonn Conference. This move certainly alienated the Pashtun majority because it transferred the government power to the Northern Alliance warlords, who were predominantly ethnic minorities. Essentially, the United States restored the same Rabbani-Masoud government that ruled Afghanistan from 1992 to 1996 in the so-called Era of Warlordism. Aside from the offense of a country (the United States) ostensibly dedicated to self-determination installing a government to rule people rather than letting those people choose their own rulers, the choice of minority rule had two historically negative echoes: it had been incompetent minority warlords who had been thrown out by the Taliban, and earlier it had been pro-Soviet Tajik Afghans who represented a foreign invader's interests. Whether there is any Pashtun bigotry in any of this, the fact remains that the history of minority rule in Afghanistan since 1979 has been viewed with extreme disfavor. For this reason alone, the restoration of the Northern Alliance warlords and Hamid Karzai was a very poor choice on the part of the United States.

Mr. Hamid Karzai was Deputy Foreign Minister in the Rabbani-Masoud Northern Alliance separatists' government. President Hamid Karzai's father was a polygamist, and his mother was from the Northern Alliance in Afghanistan. The Rabbani-Masoud government of the Northern Alliance was incompetent to rule the majority and the country was in chaos from 1992 to 1996. The Taliban overthrew the Rabbani-Masoud government in 1996.

I have been following both the USSR and the US invasions of Afghanistan. There are exact similarities between the Soviet invasion of Afghanistan in 1979 and the United States invasion of Afghanistan in 2001.

The Soviet Union invaded Afghanistan in 1979, killed the ruling President, and overthrew the Pashtun-dominated government in Afghanistan. The Kremlin appointed Babrak Karmal as president of Afghanistan and made a pro-Soviet government in Kabul. The Soviet transferred the government power from the Pashtun-dominated Khalq party to the Tajik-dominated Parchum party in Afghanistan. During the Soviet invasion, the Moscow-made regime in the 1980s in Afghanistan was simply an employee of the USSR, implementing the orders of Kremlin in Afghanistan.

Similarly, the United Sates invaded Afghanistan in 2001, overthrew the Pashtun-dominated Taliban government in Afghanistan. The White House appointed Hamid Karzai as president of Afghanistan, and made a pro-American government in Kabul. The United States transferred the government power from the majority Pashtun to the Northern Alliance minority warlords in Afghanistan. In the present US invasion, the Washington-made regime in Afghanistan is also nothing more than an employee of the US government and many of its corporations that implements the orders of the White House and CEOs in Afghanistan and in the region.

During the Soviet-Afghan War, the Soviets were friendly toward the Northern Alliance minority, but hostile toward the majority Pashtun ethnicity in Afghanistan. Over 90 percent of the Soviet's bombs were dropped in the predominantly Pashtun provinces of eastern, southern and western Afghanistan during the decade-long Soviet-Afghan War.

Similarly, the United States is currently friendly toward the Northern Alliance warlords, and hostile toward the majority Pashtun ethnicity in Afghanistan. Over 95 percent of the US and allied bombardments target the predominantly Pashtun provinces of eastern, southern and western Afghanistan during the present Afghan-American War.

In 1979, the Soviet Union justified the invasion of Afghanistan by claiming to support President Babrak Karmal's democratic regime in Afghanistan against the radical Islamic elements, foreign fighters, terrorists, American imperialism, and other reactionary forces that supported the Afghan insurgency. The Soviets claimed they did not want to occupy Afghanistan but to help the Afghan people to make a democratic and progressive government in Afghanistan.

Similarly, in 2001, the United States justified the invasion of Afghanistan as a struggle against terrorism and claimed that the United States supports President Hamid Karzai's government in Afghanistan against the radical Islamic Taliban, foreign fighters, terrorists, Osama bin Laden, and the Afghan insurgency. The United States claimed that they did not want to occupy Afghanistan, but to help the Afghan people to make democracy and prosperity for the Afghan people.

A total of 620,000 Soviet soldiers served and fought in Afghanistan during the ten-year Soviet-Afghan war, around 100,000 Soviet troops at anytime. During the occupation, the USSR used to encourage the Afghan mujahideen to negotiate with the Afghan government, lay down their weapons and participate in the Kabul government. The Soviet Union was trying to get support for the pro-soviet government in Kabul by the slogans of national reconciliation, new constitution, and democratic changes that were taking place in the country. During the Soviet occupation, the high-ranking officials of the Kabul government were pro-Russian Afghans and Patriotic Afghans were considered anti- revolutionaries and reactionaries.

Similarly, during the current Afghan-American war, there are around 100,000 US and its allies troops who are fighting to occupy Afghanistan. The United States is encouraging the Afghan people to negotiate with the Afghan government, lay down their weapons and participate in democratic elections. As a matter of fact, election in occupied Afghanistan is a political maneuver carried out by the United States in order to legitimize the occupation and the pro-American Northern Alliance minority government of Afghanistan. In fact, the Afghan president is chosen by the United States just like the pre-selected Hamid Karzai who was chosen two years prior to the invasion of Afghanistan in 2001 to be the next president after the Taliban. No matter who the elected president in Afghanistan is, their power is extremely limited. The Afghan president has just a symbolic role and does not have the authority to execute any important decision without the approval of the foreign invaders. During the current American occupation, the high-ranking officials of the Afghan government are collaborators, and Patriotic Afghans are considered suspicious and controversial figures by the US government. Presently Afghanistan is proportionately divided between the United States and its allies.

Regardless of the USSR's political slogans, the fact of the matter was that the USSR invaded Afghanistan to attain their specific geopolitical objectives in the region and to rule the economic and political life of the Afghan people. The Soviet army killed hundreds of thousands of Afghan people who were fighting for liberation of their country.

Currently, regardless of the US's political slogans, the fact of the matter is that the US invaded Afghanistan to attain its specific, long-term geopolitical goals, and to rule the economic and political life of the Afghan people. Similarly, the US military has killed tens of thousands of Afghan people who are fighting for liberation of their country.

# CHAPTER 11:
# THE UNITED STATES SUFFERED ONE 9/11, THE AFGHAN PEOPLE HAVE SUFFERED MULTIPLE 9/11S

After the collapse of the former USSR in early 1990s, the United States schemed to invade Afghanistan and to make a pro-American government in Kabul to serve US interests in the region. Again, the three specific elements that suggest the reality of the United States' strategic plan for the invasion of Afghanistan are:

The United States' involvement in the formation of the Taliban in 1994.
The expulsion of Osama bin Laden from Sudan to Afghanistan by the CIA in 1996.
The appointment of the pre-selected Hamid Karzai as president of Afghanistan in 2001.

In fact, the 9/11 tragedy in 2001 had nothing to do with the invasion of Afghanistan except as a pretext to go ahead with the preexisting desire to invade Afghanistan. Arab hijackers, predominantly from Saudi Arabia, committed the 9/11 tragedy. There was not a single Afghan who was involved in the 9/11 tragedy, nor has Afghanistan or any Afghan citizen been convicted in a court of law as responsible for the 9/11 attacks.

And yet, less than one month after the 9/11 attacks, the United States impatiently attacked Afghanistan. In 2001, the United States used numerous advanced military technologies for invading Afghanistan. In the first wave of attacks on October 7, 2001, the United States and Great Britain launched fifty Tomahawk cruise missiles from British and US submarines and ships and used many aircraft—including twenty-five strike aircraft and fifteen US Air Force bombers, such as B-1 Lancers, B-2 Spirits, and B-52 Stratofortresses—to topple the Taliban government in Afghanistan.

On October 7, 2001, both President George W. Bush and Prime Minister Tony Blair simultaneously confirmed the strikes on Afghanistan on national televisions. Later in the war, the United States used F/A-18 Hornet fighter-bombers while other US planes began cluster bombing in Afghanistan. During the Afghan-American War, the United States used AC-130 gunships and dropped 15,000-pound daisy cutter bombs in Afghanistan. In total, the US dropped more than 10,000 bombs, in toppling the Taliban government. The United States and its allies have been bombing and killing the Afghan people from 2001 to the present in order to attempt to rule the political and economic life of the Afghan people.

In the present Afghan-American War, the United States has proven very hostile to the Pashtun Afghans. The United States and its allies are mainly fighting with the majority Pashtun Afghans, who comprise more than 60 percent of Afghanistan's population. The Pashtun ethnicity is composed of hundreds of different tribes (such as Hotak, Durrani, Tanie, Zadran, Mangal, Zazie, Wazeer, Khatak, Marwat, Shinwarie, Kakar, Tarakie, Momand, and so forth). Generally Pashtun Afghans use their tribal name as their last names. When people have the same last name in Afghanistan, it generally means that those individuals belong to the same Pashtun tribes in Afghanistan.

Pashtun tribes function like huge extended families, and each tribe is composed of tens of thousands of people. Pashtuns are not only the majority in Afghanistan, but are also the second largest ethnicity in neighboring Pakistan, which has a population of approximately 150 million. Of the four provinces in Pakistan (Punjab, the Northwest or Frontier, Sindh, and Baluchistan), Pashtuns mostly live in the Frontier province close to the Afghan border.

Predominantly Pashtun Afghans defeated the British Empire in all the three Anglo-Afghan wars. In retaliation, the British government divided the Pashtun Afghans by the disputed Durand's line, which was an unofficial and imaginary borderline between British India and Afghanistan. Durand's line solely divided the Pashtun ethnicity on both sides of the border. It was this action by the British that led to border disputes between Afghanistan and British India in 1893. At that time, Pakistan had not been created. Pakistan was created through the partition of India in 1947 and was intended to be a predominantly Muslim country.

During the present US-led war in Afghanistan the Afghan people suffered huge casualties. I would like to put some figures of the civilian casualties during the current Afghan-American War in Afghanistan.

Between October 7, 2001 and June 3, 2003, the US bombing and Special Forces attacks killed approximately 3,500 civilians. This estimate counts only the deaths that occurred in the immediate aftermath of an explosion or shooting. This number does not count deaths and casualties that occurred later as a result of injuries sustained, or deaths that occurred as an indirect consequence of the US air strikes. The indirect deaths are those Afghans who were killed by exposure, associated illnesses, or injury sustained while in flight from war zones. Indirect deaths are estimated to be approximately twenty thousand from 2001 to 2003. Professor Marc W. Herold of the University of New Hampshire estimated that in the twenty-month period from October 7, 2001 to June 3, 2003, the total numbers of both direct and indirect deaths in Afghanistan were around 23,600.[5]

In the year 2005, around 1,700 people were killed in Afghanistan, including civilians, insurgents and security forces members (the Human Rights Commission's report about Afghan casualties).

In the year 2006, around 4,400 Afghans had been killed in Afghanistan. More than 1,000 of them were civilians (the Human Rights Commission's report about Afghans casualties).

In the year 2007, more than 7,700 people were killed in Afghanistan, including 1,980 civilians (the UNAMA, and the Human Rights Commission's report about Afghans casualties).

In September 2008, the UN Assistance Mission in Afghanistan (UNAMA) reported that 1,445 Afghan civilians had been

---

5      Several relevant articles are available at http:// pubpages.unh.edu/~mwherold/

killed in the first eight months of 2008, a 39 percent increase over the same period in 2007. On the contrary, the Afghan people claim that over 200,000 people have been killed by the US-led war since the invasion of Afghanistan. As a matter of fact in one instance, 2,000 Afghans were captured and collectively burned to death by the US and its allies forces in 2001 in Northern Afghanistan.

The reason for the high civilian casualty rate in Afghanistan is the fact that the United States and its allies kill the Afghan people in indiscriminate ways. For instance, on August 22, 2008, at least ninety Afghans were killed by a single attack, sixty of whom were children and fifteen women in Azizabad in western Afghanistan. A US AC-130 ground attack aircraft, equipped with gun and cannon, carried out the attack. The gunship is designed to lay waste to exposed targets with an indiscriminate torrent of bullets and artillery shells. Survivors of the attack described that there were repeated strikes on the houses where dozens of children were sleeping together with their parents, grandparents, uncles and aunts inside the houses. Most of the families were asleep when the shooting broke out, some sleeping out in the yards of their houses while others slept inside the rooms of their houses.

In term of civilian killings, both the United States and the extremist suicide bombers are similar in Afghanistan. The extremist groups justify the killing of innocent bystanders on the grounds that either the bystander will find their proper reward in death by going to Heaven if they were good Muslims, or to hell if they were bad or non-Muslims.

Similarly, the United States and its allies frequently bomb and kill Afghanistan people on speculation in indiscriminate ways by first bombing and killing people and only later identifying the dead bodies to know who was actually killed as a result of the air strikes. If the US-led bombardments do not kill the anti-American Afghan fighters, but kill women, children, and civilians, then the United States claims these were unintended targets and justifies the deaths as collateral damage of the war.

There are not only Islamic religious extremists, but also there are Christian religious extremists, Jewish religious extremists, non-religious extremists, liberal extremists, and conservative extremists. Extremist groups can exist even inside a single political party, as the Bush administration illustrated by being run by the most extremist group in the Republican Party.

Simply, the United States and its allies are killing the people of Afghanistan under the slogan of the "Global War on Terrorism." The US-led war in Afghanistan has killed tens of thousands Afghanistan people in the past seven years. The United States suffered one 9/11 tragedy where approximately 3,000 people died, Afghanistan people have suffered multiple 9/11 tragedies whereby tens of thousands of innocent people have been murdered so far by the United States military operations in Afghanistan. All human beings are born free and equal in dignity and rights. They don't deserve to be murdered on false pretenses.

The former Soviet Union in 1980s, the British Empire in the 19th century, and the Mongol invader Genghis Khan armies in 1220, invaded the region of Afghanistan and killed tens of thousands people, but none of them succeeded in occupying the land.

At the present time, the United States has invaded Afghanistan and killed tens of thousands of civilians. The United States has used the most destructive weapons and dropped 15,000-pound bombs in Afghanistan, which burned into ashes thousands and thousands of innocent Afghan people during the invasion. The people of Afghanistan remember their many foreign invaders, including the Mongol Genghis Khan, the British, the Soviets, and now the Americans; we know their differences from history or from memories, but in term of brutality,  there is hardly any difference between them.

I hope the United States and its allies stop the ongoing war and the brutal killing of the thousands of Afghan civilians, women, and children and respect Afghanistan's sovereignty, freedom and independence.

# CHAPTER 12:
# WOMEN IN AFGHANISTAN

The US and British governments claimed not only to fight terrorism in Afghanistan, but also to be concerned about women's oppression in Afghanistan as part of the justification for the 2001 invasion.

The oil-rich Arab countries of Saudi Arabia, Qatar, Bahrain, Oman, Kuwait, and the United Arab Emirates are ruled by single families with the military support of the US and the British governments. The only oil-rich Arab country in the region that was not controlled by the United States and Great Britain was Iraq. This, of course, is no longer the case. As a result, all of the interests of the oil-rich Arab countries in the Middle East are now proportionately divided between the USA and United Kingdom.

Prior to the 2001 invasion, the US and British governments made a tremendous amount of propaganda about women's oppression in Afghanistan, but in fact Afghan women were not as oppressed as was purported. The issue of Afghan women was exaggerated.

In January 2002, in his State of the Union address, President George W. Bush remarked, "The last time we met in this chamber, the mothers and daughters of Afghanistan were captives in their own homes, forbidden from working or going to school… Today, the women of Afghanistan are free…"

The self-proclaimed liberator of Afghan women President George W. Bush was indulging in political exaggeration. The fact is that the issue of women's rights was raised in Afghanistan as early as the 1920s during King Amanullah Khan's rule (1919–1929). Women's rights were one of the king's most important social reforms in Afghanistan after he won complete independence in the month-long, third Anglo-Afghan War with Great Britain.

After the Defeat of the British in 1919, King Amanullah became a national hero and turned his attention to reforming and modernizing Afghanistan. The ethnic Pashtun ruler Amanullah Khan was a patriotic reformer and, just like Kemal Ataturk in Turkey, initiated a period of dramatic changes in Afghanistan. Relevantly, the king promulgated a constitution that guaranteed the personal freedom and equal rights of all Afghans. One of the King Amanullah's social reforms in Afghanistan included a new dress code, which permitted women in Kabul to go unveiled, encouraged officials to wear Western dress, and discouraged the veiling and seclusion of women. According to Afghanistan's history, King Amanullah said to the Afghan people, "Religion does not require women to veil their hands, feet and faces, and tribal custom must not impose itself of the free will of the individuals."

The wife of Amanullah Khan Queen Soraya opened the first girls' school in Kabul in the early 1920s. The queen founded the first magazine for Afghan women called *Guidance for Women*.

King Amanullah's sister established a special hospital for Afghan women.

When I was a student in Kabul University from 1974 to 1981, all students regardless of gender had equal rights to access to education. There were numerous female students studying in medical school, engineering, pharmacy, agriculture, science, law, and religion in the universities and colleges of Afghanistan.

There was no specific dress code for girls. Some chose to dress in traditional Islamic clothes, and others chose to dress Western style clothes.

There were many high schools for girls throughout Afghanistan. After graduating from high school and passing the national examination, both males and females had equal rights in eligibility for admission and scholarships to study in Kabul University, Jalalabad University, and other co-educational colleges throughout the country.

I went to Kabul University after the overthrow of the Taliban government in Afghanistan and witnessed many female students dressed in traditional Islamic code, just as before, despite the fact that there was no restriction for girls to be dressed in Islamic clothing after the 2001 invasion. They were choosing to dress that way.

After the collapse of the Taliban government by the USA in 2001, the US media were signaled  by Washington DC to provide coverage of liberated people. On the ground, the TV journalists paid Afghan women to remove their tent-like garments, to throw them into a bonfire, and to parade themselves before the TV cameras in Afghanistan. After the cameras were switched off, the women promptly donned their burqas again.

Afghanistan is a Muslim country, and Islam respects women's rights and their dignity. The Islamic religion gives equal social rights for men and women alike. In Afghanistan, there were many females who were members of different political parties, including conservatives, religious, democratic, secular, and so forth. Many were working in all types of governmental offices. During the reign of King Mohammad Zahir Shah (1939–1973), Afghan women occupied high public offices and were members of the cabinet in the Afghan government. For instance, the Health Minister of Afghanistan at that time was a woman.

The US media unfairly purports that Islam oppresses women, but the allegations are purely political and not true. Islam must not be viewed based on the Taliban's rules. Islam is very supportive of women's rights and it respects their dignity. In Afghanistan's neighboring country of Pakistan, Benazir Bhutto was elected twice in the nation-wide elections as Prime Minister of Pakistan, which has a population nearly half the size of the United States. Benazir Bhutto was one of the most popular and brilliant female politicians who led the Pakistan's People's Party (PPP), and won general elections twice in Pakistan. In 1988, she led her party to victory after campaigning on a platform of "Food, Clothing, and Shelter for all." Benazir Bhutto was the first woman to lead a modern Muslim country. Prime Minister Bhutto was also a Muslim lady and always preferred to dress in traditional Islamic code, covering her head with a headscarf all the time.

Not only in Pakistan, but also in the Muslim nation of Bangladesh, women have been elected several times in nation-wide elections. If Islam oppresses women's rights, it is ironic that two Muslim nations have done what the United States has yet to accomplish.

By contrast, in the US and British-allied Muslim Kingdom of Saudi Arabia, women are extremely oppressed. I have seen this first hand. Saudi women do not have the right even to drive their own cars. Not only do the United States and Great Britain remain silent on massive women rights abuses in Saudi Arabia, they seem actively to support it, because without the military support of those governments the Saudi royal family could not continue to rule their kingdom. Because of their oil interests, the United States and Great Britain ignore much more serious human rights violations than prompted them to invade Afghanistan. Moreover, they are afraid of democratically elected governments in Saudi Arabia and other oil rich countries in the Arab Peninsula because the US and British governments think such would jeopardize their oil interests in those countries. However, I firmly believe that democratically elected governments in all oil-rich countries would benefit the United States and Great Britain. Unfortunately, the slogans of democracy, freedom and human rights are mere political rhetoric, because neither country's oil policies currently promote democracy, freedom and human rights, but only their own interests at the expense of anyone else.

# CHAPTER 13:
# THE UNITED STATES AND
# THE AFGHAN HEROIN

Since the occupation of the country by the USA in 2001, Afghanistan has reached the top of the list in supplying the world's heroin. The simultaneous increase of drugs in Afghanistan, after the occupation of the country by the United States in 2001, is an obvious and undeniable fact.

The people of Afghanistan have a rich culture. There was a saying in Afghanistan: "*Nisha-ie sarai nu sarai,*" which means, "A drug-addicted person is no man."

The present exponential increase of opium production in Afghanistan is a new phenomenon. Afghan people did not have heroin culture. Afghanistan reached to the top of the list in opium production and heroin trafficking only after the United States invaded Afghanistan in 2001.

When I was in Afghanistan, farmers could grow opium on their agricultural lands without any restriction from the government whatsoever, but majority of the people of Afghanistan voluntarily rejected the cultivation of opium in most parts of the country. When I was in high school, some farmers in Khoost province grew opium poppies on their land, but later, most voluntarily refrained from cultivating opium poppies on their lands, even though they could have without restriction. To be sure, there was opium and poppy cultivation in some parts of Afghanistan, but the country was one of the least opium producing countries in the world.

Opium production increased in Afghanistan during the Rabbani-Masoud dysfunctional government (1992-1996), which was run by the Northern Alliance warlords and infamous drug lords. Based on national statistics, during the Rabbani-Masoud government—in which Hamid Karzai was deputy foreign minister— Afghan opium production reached approximately 2,099 metric tons in 1996.

When the Taliban overthrew the Rabbani-Masoud Northern Alliance government in 1996, opium production in Afghanistan rapidly decreased. On Islamic grounds, the Taliban outlawed opium cultivation and had nearly eliminated completely in areas they controlled by 2001.

Since the 2001 US invasion, opium production has skyrocketed. The Bonn Conference selection of Hamid Karzai as the next Afghan president did not represent a new government but was rather simply a restoration of the warlords, drug lords, and other elements of the failed, discredited, and unwanted Rabbani-Masoud government.

The production of opium and smuggling of heroin has increased exponentially during the Karzai government. According to Afghanistan's opium statistics, opium production reached 6,100 metric tons in 2006, or about 93 percent of the entire world's opium supply. In 2006 alone, there was a 26 percent production increase from 2005. The amount of land under cultivation in opium poppies grew by 61 percent.

In the summer of 2006, the poppy harvest was estimated to have earned US$3 billion for its growers, equivalent to 52 percent of Afghanistan's GDP. Drug dealers made twenty times more than the opium growers, or US$60 billion.

There is overwhelming indirect evidence that the US-installed Karzai government and their CIA advisors are involved in the multi-billion dollar opium production and heroin trafficking business in Afghanistan. The Afghan people neither have the authority to control Afghanistan's borders nor do they have the resources to transfer 6,100 metric tons of opium to Europe and other profitable world markets for consumers. Afghanistan's borders are controlled by the US forces, and Karzai's government which rule the country.

But there is direct evidence as well. The Karzai government openly encourages people to increase opium production in Afghanistan. The governor of Kandahar province, who is the right-hand man for President Karzai, has stated persistently, "The people of Kandahar are permitted to grow opium poppies on the roofs of their houses." It is also widely rumored that one of President Karzai's brothers is also one of the top drug lords in Afghanistan. Whether this is true or not, it is the impression that Karzai's government gives to the people of Afghanistan.

The rate of growth of the opium business in Afghanistan is directly related to the profits made from the drugs made with it. Two governments have ruled Afghanistan since the invasion in 2001. The master government of Afghanistan is the United States, which dictates rules from Washington DC to Afghanistan. The second government is Karzai's puppet-government, installed by the United States and serving the interests of its foreign masters.

This $60 billion industry is having devastating and catastrophic costs on the life of the Afghan people. It is estimated that Afghanistan, with a population of twenty-five million, may now have as many as five hundred thousand heroin addicts, while the spread of HIV and AIDS is spreading as a result of the heroin addiction. Afghan people are victims of this multi-billion dollar scheme that benefits both Hamid Karzai's and the United States government's drug lords.

I left Afghanistan in 1981. When I was in Afghanistan, there were no drug addicts in the country, and most of the Afghan people did not know what heroin was, except for professionals like medical doctors and pharmacists. The now ready availability of heroin has created thousands of new drug addicts in Afghanistan, and the growing spread of lethal diseases of HIV/AIDS is the direct consequences of the new drug industry upon Afghanistan people.

The history of Afghanistan shows that the country was one of the lowest opium-producing countries in the world. This was so even when occupied by the Soviet Union from 1979 to 1989. During the decade-long Soviet-Afghan War, the level of opium production was as same as before the invasion. Now, Afghanistan is the biggest opium-producing and heroin-trafficking country in the world.

The United States is not only the world's largest oil consumer, but also the world's largest narcotic and drugs consumer as well. The CIA involvement in Afghanistan's drug trafficking is not a new phenomenon, but has a long history. Based on my personal knowledge, during the Soviet-Afghan War in 1980s, the CIA, together with the Zia-ul-Haq military regime in Pakistan, was involved in drug trafficking. An American told me this. After disclosing this information, I became concerned for his safety because he didn't know any local languages and was not familiar with the local people. I suggested that he would one day be in trouble. But he laughed and told me that not to worry because he was not alone in his drug trafficking; he and his brother, who worked for the CIA, were involved in drug-trafficking in Afghanistan together with Pakistan's Zia-ul-Haq regime. He then explained to me how, after transporting Afghanistan's drugs to one of Pakistan's port, the drugs were then loaded by Zia's own naval army personnel on Pakistani naval ships and were distributed to the world markets.

In fact, it is relatively difficult to smuggle the thousands of tons of drugs from Afghanistan through either the western border into the Islamic Republic of Iran or through the northern border of Afghanistan into multiple central Asian and eastern countries of Europe to reach the west. Transportation of Afghanistan's drugs through Pakistan and then the Indian Ocean is much easier. Even more so when most of the ground logistic transportations for the US forces in Afghanistan takes place through Pakistan and to the Indian Ocean. In other words, the majority of the Afghan heroin is exported via Pakistan to the Indian Ocean, the main route which is used by the United States military for the majority of ground logistic transportations.

The American informant told me about his involvement in the drug trafficking in Afghanistan in the mid-1980s. General Zia-ul-Haq was president and military ruler of Pakistan from July 1977 to August 1988. Zia-ul-Haq had been trained and had a military education in the United States from 1962 to1964 at the US Army Command and General Staff College at Fort Leavenworth, Kansas. He came to power after overthrowing Prime Minister Zulfikar Ali Bhutto in a military coup d'état on July 5, 1977 and became the state's third ruler to impose martial law. Prime Minister Zulfikar Ali Bhutto was executed by General Zia-ul-Haq's regime. He was founder of the Pakistan's People's Party (PPP) and the father of Prime Minister Benazir Bhutto, one of the most charismatic female politicians in Pakistan.

In the United States, it is often considered a 'conspiracy theory' to suggest that the CIA is involved in heroin trade. One might also think that the frankness of this American heroin dealer is unlikely, but in fact it illustrates how openly it was practiced. In any case, I would pose the question: can one seriously believe that 6,100 metric tons of opium were exported from Afghanistan, with how many growing fields and many heroin production facilities in Afghanistan now operating on Hamid Karzai's and the United States government's watch, and both know nothing about it?

Based on the foregoing, I predict the problem of opium production and heroin trafficking in Afghanistan will continue in the country as long as the current occupation continues.

# CHAPTER 14:
# THE COMPARISON OF
# THE USSR AND THE US
# INVASIONS

I am well aware and well informed about the situations in Afghanistan both during the time of the present US and past USSR invasions of Afghanistan. And while occupation is occupation so that there is no good occupation one would welcome (unless you are a puppet ruler), nevertheless I would like to contrast the two invasions in Afghanistan briefly as follows:

| Soviet Invasion (1979–1989) | US Invasion (2001–?) |
|---|---|
| The Soviet Union toppled the ruling government in Afghanistan, and replaced it with the pro-Soviet Karmal regime in Kabul. | The United States toppled the Taliban's government, and replaced it with the pro-American Karzai regime in Kabul. |
| Corruption and bribery was less than 10 percent | Corruption and bribery is more than 90 percent |

| Soviet Invasion (1979–1989) | US Invasion (2001–?) |
|---|---|
| Opium production and trafficking were fairly controlled, and there was no evidence that the Soviet's army or the Soviet-backed regime in Kabul was involved in the illegal drug production or drug trafficking. | Opium production and trafficking exponentially increased. Afghanistan presently supplies over 90 percent of the world's heroin. There is evidence that both the Karzai regime and the invaders are directly involved in drug production and drug trafficking |
| During the ten-year-long Afghan-Soviet war, the Red Army was relatively respectful to the Afghan culture and respected Afghan traditions most of the time. | During the Afghan-American war-to-date the United States and its allies have been arrogant toward and disrespectful of Afghan culture, and have violated it often. In Afghanistan's culture, some offenses are serious, inexcusable crimes that are punishable by death. The US military arrogantly and often commits these most serious offenses against the Afghan people. |
| The Soviets deposed the majority ethnic Pashtun government in Kabul and transferred power to the minority Tajik ethnicity. The Red Army was very hostile to the majority Pashtun ethnicity in Afghanistan. Over 90 percent of Russian aerial bombardments targeted predominantly Pashtun areas in Afghanistan. | The United States deposed the predominantly Pashtun Taliban and transferred power to the Northern Alliance of Tajik-Uzbek-Hazarah warlords in Afghanistan. The US and British armies are very hostile to the majority Pashtun ethnicity. Over 95 percent of aerial bombardments have targeted predominantly Pashtun areas in Afghanistan. |

| Soviet Invasion (1979–1989) | US Invasion (2001–?) |
|---|---|
| Most of the high government officials of Babrak Karmal's regime were popular politicians and had non-criminal histories in Afghanistan. | Most of the high government officials of Hamid Karzai's regime are either outsiders and unpopular in Afghanistan, or are notorious warlords with criminal histories in the country. |
| The Red Army coordinated with the Soviet-backed Karmal regime in Afghanistan and listened to the recommendations and comments of Afghan military officers during military operations. Consequently, civilian casualties as a result of air bombardments were relatively low. | US and allied forces do not fight in coordination with the US-backed Karzai government in Afghanistan. The United States and its allies do not heed the recommendations and comments of Afghan military officers. Consequently, civilian casualties as a result of air bombardments are high. Frequently, the United States and its allies have targeted civilians, including women and children, at wedding ceremonies, residential areas and mosques.<br><br>US and allied forces are not only arrogant about this, but also do not acknowledge the wrongdoing and incidents involving civilian casualties. Instead, they try to justify the killing of Afghan civilians by denials or cover-ups. |

| Soviet Invasion (1979–1989) | US Invasion (2001–?) |
|---|---|
| The Soviets helped the Afghan people to rebuild Afghanistan and spent money in a very transparent way in order to win the hearts and minds of the Afghan people during the occupation. | The international community has sent billions of dollars to Afghanistan, but almost all the international assistance was stolen by the pro-US Karzai government. The billions of dollars in aid poured into Afghanistan have neither helped the Afghan people nor were spent to rebuild the country.<br><br>Furthermore, there are thousands of Afghan-American collaborators working in Afghanistan to consolidate the US occupation, but their monthly salaries are being deposited in US banks by the US government. The Afghan-American collaborators receive only 10 percent of their salaries; the rest is deposited in the United States, perhaps so that their money cannot be spent in Afghanistan to help the Afghan's economy. |
| There were massive human rights abuses in jails against the Afghans who were fighting to liberate Afghanistan from the Soviet's invasion, but there was no evidence that Afghan people were being bitten or killed by dogs then. | Massive human rights abuses are occurring in the jails, both against civilians and those Afghans who are fighting to liberate Afghanistan. There is evidence of entire Afghan families being bitten and killed by dogs. |

# CHAPTER 15:
# THE VITAL STEPS TO A SUSTAINABLE PEACE IN AFGHANISTAN

To make peace in Afghanistan, it would be better to look at the history of Afghanistan and learn from the past. The history of Afghanistan undoubtedly teaches three lessons.

Foreign invaders cannot occupy Afghanistan.

All puppet regimes made by invaders have failed to rule the Afghan people. Only governments made by the Afghan people can rule Afghanistan.

The defeat of the Afghan governments by foreign invaders does not mean the controlling of the Afghan people.

The first historic lesson from the Afghan history is that none of the foreign invaders have succeeded in occupying Afghanistan. Geographically, Afghanistan is the crossroad to Asia and has important geopolitical locations. Historically, many of the world's empires and superpowers have invaded Afghanistan.

Multiple bloody wars have been fought between the foreign invaders and the people of Afghanistan. But none of the foreign invaders have succeeded in occupying Afghanistan.

During the first Anglo-Afghan War (1839–1842), the British invaded and installed Shah Shuja's pro-British regime in Kabul. The British voiced no intention to occupy Afghanistan, but claimed only that they wished to help Shah Shuja's government in Afghanistan. This trick fooled no one. After heavy fighting between the British and Afghan people, the British army was defeated and was driven out of Afghanistan in 1842. Shah Shuja was assassinated in Kabul as soon as the British Empire left. During the second Anglo-Afghan War (1878–1880), again the British failed to occupy Afghanistan. With the third Anglo-Afghan War (1919), the British were defeated once and for all, and Afghanistan achieved full independence.

During the Soviet-Afghan War (1979–1989), the USSR invaded Afghanistan for specific geopolitical reasons. The ruling president of Afghanistan was killed and Karmal's pro-Soviet regime was established in Kabul. The Soviet's strongest mechanical army was defeated despite the fact that a total of 620,000 Soviet soldiers were deployed in the decade-long war, and despite having 1200 kilometers of shared border in common. When Babrak Karmal proved unable to consolidate his government, the General Secretary of the Soviet Communist Party Mikhail Gorbachev removed him from power replaced him with Dr. Najibullah in November 1986. Although President Najibullah adopted a new constitution and a policy of national reconciliation, his regime also failed because it was obviously installed by USSR.

During the current US-Afghan War (2001–), the United States and its allies toppled a stabilizing Pashtun Afghan government and installed the pro-US Karzai government in Kabul. Like President Karmal, President Karzai has been unable to consolidate his government in the eight years since the US invaded. His hold on power has at times been so slight that he has mockingly been referred to not as president, but as the mayor of Kabul.

The second historic lesson from Afghan history is that all puppet regimes made by invaders have failed to rule Afghan people. Only governments made by the Afghan people could rule Afghanistan.

Before the Soviet invasion, Afghan governments ruled the Afghan people without special difficulties. King Mohammad Zahir Shah (1933–1973) ruled Afghanistan peacefully for forty years; President Daoud Khan (1973–1978) ruled Afghanistan peacefully.

After its invasion, the USSR was unable to rule the Afghan people, despite the presence of the Soviet's huge army and their sophisticated weapons. Both King Mohammad Zahir Shah and President Daoud were less powerful than the Soviet's Red Army, but had no difficulty ruling. The USSR could not rule Afghanistan simply because they were invaders. Freedom is paramount for Afghan people. They like their freedom and cannot be oppressed and ruled by invaders or those invaders' installed regimes.

Before the US invasion, the Taliban had secured most of the country in the span of a few years and overthrew Rabbani-Masoud's Northern Alliance government in 1996. The Taliban defeated the warlords and cleaned up Afghanistan village by village, town by town, and province by province until within five years they had restored peace and security to 95 percent of the country. By contrast, the United States and their allies have failed to restore peace and security in Afghanistan over the past eight years, and the end is nowhere in sight. At times, their installed puppet, President Karzai, could barely even rule the city of Kabul alone.

The Taliban were not stronger than the United States' and its allies' forces, but the Taliban were from Afghanistan and knew the Afghan culture, traditions, languages, religion, history and customs. They knew how to deal with the Afghan people and how to rule the Afghan people. The US cannot and will not rule Afghanistan simply because they are invaders. Afghan people like their freedom and will not be oppressed and ruled by invaders or those invaders' installed regimes.

Regardless of the slogans behind the invasions, the Afghan people do not differentiate between the British, Russian, or US invasions of Afghanistan. Afghan people are fighting for their freedom against the United States and its allies just as they did against the British and Russian invaders of the past.

The third historic lesson from the Afghan history is that the defeat of the Afghan governments by foreign invaders does not mean the controlling of the Afghan people.

The British invaded Afghanistan and defeated the Afghan government temporarily in 1839. They established the pro-British government of Shah Shuja in Kabul but did not control the Afghan people.

The Soviet Union invaded Afghanistan and defeated the Amin government in 1979. They installed the pro-Soviet government of Babrak Karmal in Kabul but did not control the Afghan people.

The United States and its allies invaded Afghanistan and defeated the Taliban government in 2001. They established the pro-US government of Hamid Karzai in Kabul but have not controlled the Afghan people.

The conclusion is obvious to draw.

From the foregoing three historic lessons, it should be clear to the United States that the best way to make peace in Afghanistan is to stop trying to reach its geopolitical goals by forcing an occupation upon the people of Afghanistan. The USSR was in the verge of economic collapse after the decade long Soviet-Afghan War. Now the current world economic climate may put the United States in a similar position. Regardless, war is expensive in Afghanistan. The United States and its allies cannot pay the huge economic expense of war in Afghanistan for an indefinite length of time. It is in their self-interest to follow a path to peaceful resolutions in order to end the present Afghan-American War. The following steps will end or considerably decrease the ongoing violence in Afghanistan:

> The greatest periods of stability and security have been at times when Pashtun Afghans rule Afghanistan. This is doubtless because the majority of people in Afghanistan are Pashtun Afghans. But this does not mean minority Afghans cannot rule in peace and security. It does mean, however, that they cannot rule as puppets of foreign invaders or with selfish self-interest in mind, as the Northern Alliance separatists did. As a historic fact, the Pashtun Afghans have ruled Afghanistan almost continuously since its birth in 1747. Afghanistan has been ruled by Pashtun Afghans in the past over 250 years. Recently, Afghanistan was ruled only for almost ten years by non-Pashtun rulers: Habibullah Kalakani, President Babral Karmal, and

President Burhanudin Rabbani. All three were Tajik Afghans.

The USA and its allies should minimize confrontation with Afghan people and avoid direct fighting as much as they can for the simple reason that killing Afghan people by occupiers is not only futile but increases violence and retaliation. The United States and its allies cannot stabilize Afghanistan by only military means and fighting against the Afghan people. If military solutions cannot be avoided—and they must be—then military intervention by Muslim countries would at least be more acceptable to Afghan people.

President Karzai and his Northern Alliance government are discredited in its entirety and should be replaced with a more acceptable government because the Afghan people consider President Karzai illegitimate and unworthy of following.

In any presidential election in Afghanistan the dominant role should be played by the United Nations, not the United States and its allies given that the United States and its allies are directly involved in fighting and killing of Afghan people. Afghan people are more hostile to the United States and its allies because they have killed tens of thousands of Afghan people since the invasion in 2001. The United Nations should support the most popular Afghan candidates—those who are in close contact with Afghan people—and not outsiders who live in the United States or its allies' countries.

All the notorious warlords in the Karzai government should be removed from public office for the reason that those warlords were involved in massive human rights abuses for many years in Afghanistan. Politically, these warlords may be acceptable to the United States and its allies as official parts of the Afghan government, but they are unacceptable to the Afghan people for the many, deeply offensive crimes they have committed against civilians in Afghanistan.

President Karzai himself, and his top government officials should be prosecuted for stealing billions of dollars of international aid, which was donated for the rebuilding of Afghanistan. Such prosecutions not only will improve the image of the Afghan government, but will also send a positive message to the Afghan people at large. Those billions of dollars robbed and stolen by President Karzai and his top officials should be returned to the Afghan people, since they are very much needed.

Democracy must be the rule of majority. Afghanistan can be ruled mainly by the majority with the usual proportion of all other minor ethnicities just as in the past. After the collapse of the Taliban government, the Bush administration alienated the majority Pashtun ethnicity by imposing the Northern Alliance minority warlords on Afghanistan. That minority was not only undemocratic, but also ignored the historic fact that minority governments have never ruled Afghanistan effectively or stabilized the country.

Afghans are proud of their rich and noble culture. Afghanistan can be ruled by a strong central government based on Afghan traditions and culture. Afghanistan cannot be ruled by externally imported rules and regulations. There are many things in foreign legal systems that are unacceptable to Afghan people because they are at odds with Afghan culture. To mention just two examples: homosexuality is lawful in the US legal system, and is even constitutional in some US states. Nudity also is legal in many areas in the United States. Nude dancing is legal in specific areas in United States. Both homosexuality and nudity are considered immoral and absolutely unacceptable in the Islamic culture of Afghanistan. Afghanistan can be ruled successfully only by the Afghan people based on the traditionally accepted rules, values, and the Afghan culture as before. Afghan people respect and prefer their culture to externally imposed rules. For this reason, all foreigners who live in the country should respect Afghan culture. Any law or provision that contradicts the Afghan culture should be discarded from Afghanistan's constitution because it provokes resistance and disobedience.

Contrary to the United States legal and judicial system, Afghan culture is straightforward and honest. All wrongdoings, mistakes, and obvious facts should be acknowledged honestly even if they are harmful and not in the favor of the wrongdoers. In the Afghan culture, honestly acknowledged wrongdoings and mistakes are forgivable, but dishonest denial of wrongdoings is unforgivable. Denial of wrongdoings, mistakes, and obvious facts increases distrust between the Afghan people and the foreigners. For instance, the United States and its allies have bombed wedding ceremonies, mosques, residential areas, civilians, women and children, and killed innocent people numerous times in Afghanistan. The United States and its allies simply deny this and try to justify the civilian causalities by either denial or covering them up. Denial of obvious facts exponentially increases anger and the desire for retaliation in Afghan people. Killing of civilians, women and children by the United States and its allies' forces should not be covered up or denied but should be acknowledged honestly. Honesty pays off in Afghan culture.

Generally, US, UK, and Israeli governments' officials are not welcomed in the Muslim world for the reason that they are seen as participating in their governments' anti-Islamic policies, and particularly the continued, US and UK supported occupation of the Al-Aqsa mosque in East Jerusalem, which is the third holiest mosque in the Islam religion. In the Islamic world the AAIA is considered anti-Islamic alliance. The government officials of those countries, and especially Israel, are considered enemies of Islam in the Islamic world. For this reason, American-Jewish politicians who are notorious in the Muslim world like Senator Joe Liebermann should not go to Afghanistan because it would be seen as provocative and would send a wrong message to Afghan people, inadvertently or not. Afghan people do not want Afghanistan to be a second Palestine or be under siege like the Gaza strip.

Respect of Afghan culture is extremely important in building relations with Afghan people. In Afghanistan, Afghan culture is stronger than the law. Afghan culture is a school of specific traditions that are accepted in the Afghan society. Afghan people obey these traditional rules voluntarily without enforcement. Any violation of the Afghan culture has severe impact and consequences. To be effective in Afghanistan, one must have an understanding of and respect for Afghan culture. For instance, just to mention a few Afghan culture is affronted by guards who insult prisoners in captivity and jails, by people who show disrespect to sacred things, people who disrespect the elderly, women and children, and by those who use disproportionate military force and heavy handed tactics.

The solution of the Durand problem is essential for stability in the region and to quell the violence in the semi-autonomous Pashtuns' areas and the Northwest Pashtuns' province of Pakistan. Pashtun Afghans are always the major part of resistance against the foreign invasions, and play pivotal role in freedom and independence. The Durand Line divides the major Pashtun ethnicity on both sides of the border. The Durand problem was created by the British Empire in 1893, when the British India was defeated by the Pashtun warriers.

Implementing these recommendations will be key to restoring peace or at least to considerably decrease the present violence in Afghanistan. They are vital for making a sustainable and durable peace in the country.

# CHAPTER 16:
# THE ISLAMIC WORLD AND THE ANGLO-AMERICAN-ISRAELI ALLIES

There is no doubt that there is a long-term hostility between the United States, Great Britain, the Israeli and the Muslim world.

Approximately 25 percent of the world's population is Muslims. Based on the census taken in 2007, in total there are approximately 1.78 billion Muslims in the World. There are 46 Muslim countries and 56 Muslim minority countries in the World. Muslims comprise approximately 2.5 percent of the United States' population.

The fundamental reason for the hostility between the Islamic world and the United States, Great Britain, and Israeli governments is the issue of the occupation of the Al-Aqsa Mosque in East Jerusalem since 1967. It is the third holiest place in Islam.

Religiously, the first holiest place is Al-Haram in Mecca, in the Kingdom of Saudi Arabia. The second holiest place is Al-

Masjid Al-Nabawi or the Prophet's Mosque in Medina, in the Kingdom of Saudi Arabia. Al-Masjid Al-Nabawi stands on the site of a mosque built by the Holy Prophet Muhammad himself next to his house and contains the Prophet's tomb. The third holiest place in Islam is Al-Aqsa in East Jerusalem, which has been occupied by Israel since 1967 with the support of the United States and British governments.

As a historical fact, in 1917, the British occupied Jerusalem. Jerusalem was the capital of Palestine until 1948. From 1949, Jerusalem was divided into Israel and Arab sectors. Jerusalem was divided until 1967 when Israel, with the help of the United States, annexed all of Jerusalem including the Al-Aqsa Mosque following the Six Day War.

Muslim people believe the occupation of the Holy Mosque of Al-Aqsa by Israel with the military and financial support of the United States and the British government is much more than just a political offense. It is a religious offense of the highest order. Imagine the offense to Christianity if the Holy Grail was regularly defiled by another religion. Because the Al-Aqsa Mosque is daily occupied, all who participate in that occupation and make it possible are seen as anti-Muslim allies. Because of this offense, the United States government is seen as the number one enemy of Islam in the world.

There are more than one and a half billion Muslims in the world. Generally, all Muslims in the entire world are unhappy with the policies that support AAIA occupation of Islam's third holiest site. However the Islamic radical parties in Muslim countries are more hostile to AAIA governments than mainstream Muslims for the reason that the liberation of the Al-Aqsa Mosque in East Jerusalem is one of their primary goals.

I was a student at Kabul University from 1974 to 1981. The members of the Islamic Brotherhood parties used to debate the liberation of Al-Aqsa Mosque in East Jerusalem as an Islamic duty for any Muslim in the world. The liberation of Al-Aqsa Mosque is one of the primary goals of the Islamic brotherhood parties and one of the top Islamic items for lobbying others to join the radical parties.

In addition to Afghanistan, I was in Pakistan and Saudi Arabia during the Soviet-Afghan War in the 1980s. Most of the Muslim radical parties were hostile toward the AAIA governments and considered the liberation of the Al-Aqsa Mosque as one of their primary duties.

The Islamic radical parties are Islamic political organizations that politically struggle to rule their Islamic countries according to Islamic law. These Islamic radical parties operate in almost all Islamic countries like Afghanistan, Pakistan, Iran, Lebanon, Palestine, Syria, Egypt, Somalia, Yemen, and so forth. These parties have different political platforms, but all of them have a unique religious goal in common, and that is the liberation of Al-Aqsa Mosque in East Jerusalem. Improbable as it may seem, the full liberation of the Al-Aqsa Mosque will end the greatest portion of hostility between the Islamic world and AAIA governments. It would also reduce the appeals for extremist group recruitment.

A comprehensive, peaceful resolution of the Al-Aqsa Mosque situation is extremely important for peace and stability in the world. The issue of the liberation of the Al-Aqsa Mosque does not belong only to Palestinians but to the whole Islamic world.

It should be clear that Muslims are not against any country or religion in the world. The AAIA allegation that Muslims are intolerant to other religions or cultures and all hate the West is absolutely not true. These three allies are trying to involve other countries in their problem with the Islamic world. There are many non-Muslim minorities living in peace and prosperity in many Muslim-majority countries around the world.

The Muslims have only one specific issue with the AAIA governments, and that issue is the occupation of the Al-Aqsa Mosque in East Jerusalem. AAIA propaganda that the Islamic religion is against other religions or Western democracy is merely political rhetoric for lobbying other countries to joint them against Muslims. Such untrue propaganda against Islam by the AAIA allies only increases the hostility and hatred between them and the Islamic world. It is a simple fact that the hatred and animosity between the Muslim world and AAIA governments can never end until the issue of the Al-Aqsa Mosque is resolved.

The United States, Great Britain, and Israel have a unique and long-term historic and political relationship compared to the rest of the world. It is necessary to mention briefly these historic and political ties.

Around the world, there has never been a shortage of countries occupying others. Both the British Empire first, and the Soviet Empire second, are exemplary representatives on a grand scale. With the fall of the Soviet Union, the field was left essentially free for the US Empire to flourish unchallenged. Often this is called the US dominance in the world. And where once Britain was the empire, it now maintains access to imperial reach by sticking close to the new emperor, the United States. All of these empires, like most, have never shied away from killing inhabitants in desired lands, whether aborigines, or Indians east or west. And it always advanced under a glorious banner—manifest destiny, civilization, and democracy.

*Akhtar M. Qassimyar, M.D.*

This is nothing new, and the affinity between race, political systems, and religion all just further the ties between the United States and Britain, whatever else they disagree on. Mutual self-interest came together once more on May 15, 1948, with the founding of the State of Israel. The issue is not nearly so straightforward as that, but from that date there has been an ever-increasing influence of Israeli interests in US and UK politics. Besides Israel itself, the United States and Great Britain have more Jewish legislatures than any other country in the world. This is particularly striking in the United States, where Muslims and Jewish people alike make up only 2.5 percent of the population, yet the number of Muslims elected to political office are virtually negligible.

To many in the Muslim world, this tremendous representation in the politics of two of the most powerful countries in the world is sometimes referred to as a Zionist conspiracy, assisted by a Jewish-dominated, anti-Muslim media in the United States and Great Britain. But it is not necessary to say this. It is simply true that Anglo-American-Israeli political interests are now intimately intertwined. Insofar as a lessening of world tension would result from the simple act of no longer occupying the Al-Aqsa Mosque in East Jerusalem, one can only wonder not simply why this simple act has yet to happen, but why so many people in the United States are totally unaware of it. If one considers not just the Israeli, but also the Anglo-American Christian history with regard to Jerusalem, then it may no longer be a mystery.

Nevertheless, I hope that the three allies respect the Islamic world and resolve the issue of the Al-Aqsa Mosque in East Jerusalem for the reason that the full liberation of the mosque will eliminate the world-wide hostility and hatred between the over one and a half billion Muslims and the United States, British, and the Israelis governments.

# CHAPTER 17:
# THE ARAB WORLD AND THE ANGLO-AMERICAN-ISRAELI ALLIES

By looking at history, we learn that in 1897 the first Zionist Congress at Basle, Switzerland approved the concept of Jewish nationalism to establish a Jewish State. The British government supported it. The British government then implemented the plan to make a Jewish state in the land of Palestine. The British occupied Palestine and Jerusalem in November 1917. From that movement, Jewish immigration from Europe started to Palestine with the British cabinet pledged in support of a Jewish homeland. During the 1930s, the displacement of the Arab population began.

As part of the Jews' plan to terrorize the Arab population, on April 9, 1948, the Irgun and Lehi Jewish gangs carried out the massacre of more than 200 Palestinian villagers, including old people, women and children in West Jerusalem. The Palestinian people lived in peace, when the groups, supported by the Anglo-American allies, attacked them in their own land.

Irgun and Lehi's attack on April 9, 1948 caused widespread panic amongst Palestinians and they fled from their homes across the country. Just a month later, on May 15, 1948, Israel was declared a state and was recognized by the United States of America the same day. By mid 1949, 750,000 out of 900,000 Palestinian Arabs had left the affected region, forced out by the Israeli terror tactics.

Jerusalem was the capital of Palestine until 1948. From 1949, Jerusalem was divided between Israeli and Palestinian parts. In 1967, the Israel, supported by United States and Great Britain, annexed the entire Palestinian territories of Gaza, the West Bank, and East Jerusalem, including the Al-Aqsa Mosque during the Six Day War. On June 28, 1967, the Israeli government annexed the occupied Palestinian territories into the state of Israel itself.

From 1917 to the present time, the Israel has committed numerous atrocities to Palestinian people in Palestine. The Palestinians are fighting against the Israel in order to liberate Palestinian territory occupied by the Israeli regime.

Historically, Israelis and Palestinians are cousins. Israelis are Jews, speak Hebrew, and their religion is Judaism. Palestinians are Arabs, speak Arabic language, and their religion is Islam.

The Palestinian people are supported by the Arab people in many Arab countries in their struggle to liberate their occupied Palestine from the Israel. There are twenty-two Arab countries in the world namely: Algeria, Bahrain, Chad, Comoros, Egypt, Iraq, Jordan, Kuwait, Lebanon, Libya, Mauritania, Morocco, Oman, Palestine, Qatar, Saudi Arabia, Somalia, Sudan, Syria, Tunisia, United Arab Emirates, and Yemen. Currently, the Arab population is around 320 million.

The United States and Great Britain are the two most supportive governments of Israel in the world partly because the United States and Great Britain have the highest numbers of Jewish legislators outside of Israel, but also because the three governments have distinguished political, historical and economical relations and common interests in Jerusalem and the Middle East, if not the rest of the world.

Briefly, the hatred between Arabs and the AAIA governments is clear and reflected in the occupation of Palestinian-Arab land. The hatred and animosity between Arab people and the AAIA will exist as long as the occupation of the Palestinian's land persists.

Over 320 million Arab people support the Palestinians and their nation because all Arabs are historical brothers and have the same language, the same religion, and the same culture regardless of their different citizenships. The Arabs support the Palestinian people in their struggle for independence. In the September 11 tragedy in 2001, all the hijackers who committed suicide attacks in the United States were Arab people from different Arab countries, with a majority from Saudi Arabia. The reason for such hatred is clear but can be resolved by ending the occupation of the Palestinian territory of West Bank, Gaza Strip, and East Jerusalem, which has been occupied by Israel with the support of the United States and Great Britain since 1967.

Since the occupation of Palestine in 1967, thousands of Palestinian civilians, women and children have been massacred by the Israelis with the full support of the US and British governments. Despite the massacres of the Palestinian people in the past several decades, the Zionist regime of Israelis has failed in its entirety to extinguish the determination of the Palestinian people for an independent Palestinian State.

I believe it is in the best interests of the AAIA governments to end the occupation and give back to the Palestinian people the right to make an independent Palestinian State on their homeland side by side with Israel.

# CHAPTER 18:
# AL-QAEDA AND THE ANGLO-AMERICAN-ISRAELI ALLIES

Al-Qaeda is an Arab nationalist organization that fights for Arab causes. The Al-Qaeda network is not only fighting for the Palestine's liberation, but also for the withdrawal of the US and British military from Saudi Arabia and other oil-rich countries in the Arab Peninsula (listed below). Single ruling families with the military support of the United States and British governments govern six of the oil-rich Arab countries: Saudi Arabia, Kuwait, Bahrain, Qatar, Oman, and the United Arab Emirates.

I was in Saudi Arabia for almost eight years working in the Ministry of Health. The ruling royal family in the Kingdom of Saudi Arabia owns almost the entire country. It seems as if everything in the Kingdom of Saudi Arabia belongs to the royal family, including entire oil revenue, the natural resources, the lands, and so forth. Almost all of the universities, highways, airports, hospitals, and so forth in Saudi Arabia carry the names of the members of the Saudi royal family: King Abdulaziz University, King Khalid International Airport, King Fahd Hospital, King Faisal Specialist Hospital, along with numerous other names of members of the Saudi royal family that are too plentiful and too boring.

There is neither election nor democracy in Saudi Arabia. The people of Saudi Arabia are extremely oppressed by the members of the royal family. The Saudi government is ruled by a single family, and is one of the most oppressive and dictatorial governments in the world. Women have no right to drive their own cars in Saudi Arabia.

The United States, Great Britain, and the governing families in the oil-rich countries in the Arab peninsula serve the interests of each other at the expense of the oppression and suffering of the millions of people in those countries. The people in the Arab peninsula are hostile to the United States and British governments for the reason that they believe that the dictatorial single families could not rule and oppress the people in the US-dominated oil-rich countries without the military support of the US and the British governments.

I believe the current Al-Qaeda and AAIA conflict will end if the AAIA governments end the occupation of Palestine and if the US and British governments promote democracy instead of supporting single-family rule in Saudi Arabia, Kuwait, Bahrain, Qatar, Oman, and the United Arab Emirates.

The killing or capturing of Osama Bin Laden, his lieutenants, or hundreds or thousands of other people affiliated with the Al-Qaeda organization will not resolve the ongoing war between Al-Qaeda and the AAIA governments.

Al-Qaeda is very influential, not only in Saudi Arabia, Kuwait, Bahrain, Qatar, Oman, and the United Arab Emirates, but also throughout all twenty-two Arab countries. When September 11 tragedy happened in the United States, many people in the

Middle East were dancing in the streets because the people in Saudi Arabia, Kuwait, Bahrain, Qatar, Oman, the United Arab Emirates, Egypt, and Jordan, are all oppressed by their ruling governments supported by the US and British governments.

I believe Al-Qaeda is a product of oppression not a product of democracy. If there were democratically elected governments in Saudi Arabia, Kuwait, Bahrain, Qatar, Oman, UAE, and Jordan instead of single-family governments, the Al-Qaeda organization would not be able to recruit people in the Arab peninsula and other Arab countries so readily and, as a result, Al-Qaeda would virtually disappear by itself. The United States and Great Britain would benefit more from democratically elected governments in the region than from supporting the rule of the single family governments in the Arab peninsula.

Al-Qaeda is a very determined enemy of the AAIA. Al-Qaeda is not running away from confronting the AAIA governments. Al-Qaeda is always searching to fight and harm the citizens of the US, Great Britain, and Israel. It is worth pointing out that during Saddam Hussein's regime there was no Al-Qaeda in Iraq. As soon as the United States and Great Britain occupied Iraq, Al-Qaeda transferred its bases from the neighboring Arab countries in order to fight against the foreign militaries in occupied Iraq. Al-Qaeda has considerably damaged the United States and Great Britain in Iraq not only in term of human losses, but also financially as well, as the cost of the Iraq war has reached over two billion dollars in a week. On the contrary, the United States and Great Britain were trying to avoid fighting with Al-Qaeda and Arab fighters in Iraq. There were many Arab fighters from Arab countries who were pouring into Iraq in order to fight against the US and British forces, but the US and UK were begging the neighboring countries of Iraq to prevent the flow of Al-Qaeda and Arab fighters into Iraq.

Since the beginning of the war against Al-Qaeda, the organization becomes more powerful and more violent than before. As a matter of fact, currently Al-Qaeda has numerous underground activities in many countries in the world. It is extremely difficult to eradicate all those numerous secret cells and groups in the world. The ongoing war against Al-Qaeda seems to be very long and very expensive. I believe the cost-effective war against Al-Qaeda will be the promotion of democracy in the Arab peninsula, and the creation of Palestinian State.

# CHAPTER 19:
# AL-QAEDA AND THE
# TALIBAN

The United States government and its media purport that both the Taliban and Al-Qaeda are the same, but in fact, they are not the same and differ in many ways.

The Taliban are Afghan religious clerics, not a secret organization. The Taliban ruled Afghanistan from 1996 to 2001. Al-Qaeda is an international, underground Arab organization that has yet to rule any government. The Taliban and Al-Qaeda are not the same, and there further obvious differences between them.

The Taliban Movement in Afghanistan is an Afghan clergy class that is composed of both mullahs of mosques (religious clerics) and Islamic religious students (the Taliban). The scope of their activities is limited to inside Afghanistan or neighboring Pakistan.

By contrast, Al-Qaeda is an Arab organization and has pure Arab agenda. Al-Qaeda was founded by Osama bin Laden. To review for the sake of clarity, Osama bin Laden is a civil engineer and graduated from King Abdulaziz University in Saudi Arabia. During the Soviet Union's invasion of Afghanistan in the 1980s, he and his group helped the Afghan mujahideen together with the US government to liberate Afghanistan. When he returned victoriously to his country of Saudi Arabia in 1989 following the defeat and withdrawal of the Soviet army from Afghanistan, he became dissatisfied with the US military presence there.

Osama bin Laden was a close friend of the United States during the Soviet-Afghan War, but that friendship broke up when Osama openly stated his opposition to the US military presence in Saudi Arabia. The ruling royal family of Saudi Arabia expelled Osama from his own country of Saudi Arabia, and Osama moved to Sudan in 1992 where he founded Al-Qaeda in order to fight for the withdrawal of the US and British military from Saudi Arabia and the other oil-rich countries in the Arab peninsula. As such, Al-Qaeda's political objectives are purely related to Arab issues. The Al-Qaeda's two main goals are:

To Fight against the United States and British government for the withdrawal of their military forces from the oil-rich Arab countries of Saudi Arabia, Kuwait, Bahrain, Qatar, Oman, and the UAE.

To liberate the Arab land of Palestine from US and British-supported Israeli occupation.

In other words, Al-Qaeda is an anti-American, anti-British, and anti-Israeli organization that has global activities in multiple countries, not limited to Afghanistan.

The scope of the Taliban activities is limited to Afghanistan and neighboring Pakistan where the Taliban attended the same religious schools (madrasas). The scope of the Al-Qaeda activities is worldwide, and not limited to a single country.

The Taliban movement began with the help of the United States after the collapse of the Soviet-backed Najibullah government in Afghanistan in the 1990s, and was supported financially and militarily by the US and its allies to defeat the four anti-American radical Islamic Brotherhood parties in Afghanistan.

In contrast, Al-Qaeda was founded by Osama bin Laden. It has been anti-American, anti-British, and anti-Israeli since its foundation and fights against US and British military presence or occupation in Arab states.

The animosity between the Taliban and the United States started when the US toppled the Taliban government of Afghanistan in 2001. The Taliban have been fighting against the United States and its allies inside Afghanistan since that time.

Al-Qaeda, on the other hand, is always in search of an arena to fight against the United States of America and its allies everywhere in the world. For example, prior to the US invasion of Iraq, there was no Al-Qaeda there. It was only after the occupation of Iraq by the United States and Britain that Al-Qaeda transferred its bases to Iraq in order to fight against the United States and Britain governments.

When the Soviet Union invaded Afghanistan in 1979, the Afghanistan people including the Afghan clergies, mullahs, the Taliban, Osama bin Laden and other foreign Muslim volunteers from Arab and non-Arab countries fought with the help of the United States government to liberate Afghanistan from Soviet invasion. In the same way, many Afghan people perceive the present invasion of Afghanistan by the United States and its allies as an occupation of their country, and they are fighting for their liberation just as they did against the Soviet invasion of Afghanistan in the 1980s. The Taliban do not target the AAIA interests in the world. They fight only against the United States inside Afghanistan to liberate their own country.

In 2001, the United States toppled the Taliban government for their alleged involvement with the September 11 tragedy. The Taliban are Afghans and have only an Afghanistan agenda in mind. The Taliban believe their government was legitimate, especially since not a single Afghan was involved in the September 11 tragedy in the United States. Moreover, the Taliban has not been charged or convicted in a court of law as being involved in the September 11 tragedy in any way. The Taliban believe that the United States and British governments toppled their legitimate government in Afghanistan in 2001 without justification.

The Taliban is not Al-Qaeda. They are absolutely different from Al-Qaeda. If Afghanistan's issue is resolved, the animosity between the United States and the Taliban will be over, but the animosity between Al-Qaeda and the AAIA will continue because it is unrelated to Afghanistan.

The Taliban is a religious class in Afghan society that leads prayers in mosques, attends funeral ceremonies, resolves civil disputes between people, and so forth. But Al-Qaeda is a global Arab nationalist underground network that has activities in multiple countries, including twenty-two Arab countries, and that receives financial support especially from people in the oil-rich Arab countries.

At the present time, the Taliban and the Al-Qaeda organization have a common objective: fighting against the United States and its allies in Afghanistan. But it should be clarified that the Taliban and Al-Qaeda are fighting against the United States for different purposes and reasons. The Taliban are fighting to force the withdrawal of the United States from Afghanistan and to restore sovereignty of their country. In contrast, Al-Qaeda is fighting against the United States and its allies in Afghanistan for other reasons, which include Arab issues beyond sampling ousting the United States and its allies from Afghanistan. In other words, if the United States occupies any country other than Afghanistan, Al-Qaeda will fight against the US in that occupied country as well. The Taliban hostility against the United States, by contrast, is limited to Afghanistan, and does not include Arab issues. Afghan Muslims may share Al-Qaeda's anger at the occupation of the Al-Aqsa Mosque, but this does not make them the same. Even formerly bitter enemies, like the Taliban and the Gulboddin Hekmatyar's Hezb-ie Islamie party have set aside their differences to fight the common foe of the US and its allies in Afghanistan.

The AAIA is continuously trying to make allies in the world in order to defeat Al-Qaeda. In the same way, Al-Qaeda is also trying to make allies in the world to fight against the AAIA. Al-Qaeda seeks to find its allies in countries like Afghanistan, Iraq, Palestine, Egypt, Jordan, the Kingdom of Saudi Arabia, United Arab Emirates, Qatar, Bahrain, and other oil-rich Arab Gulf countries where people are directly or indirectly oppressed by the AAIA.

The foregoing shows how the Taliban and Al-Qaeda are not the same. Hopefully in the future it will no longer be possible for the media to present them as one for the purpose of stirring up animosity toward the Afghan people.

# CHAPTER 20:
# WHY THE SAUDI PEOPLE ARE MORE HOSTILE TO THE UNITED STATES GOVERNMENT

The Kingdom of Saudi Arabia is one of the closest allies of the United States of America in the Middle East. A royal family has ruled the government of Saudi Arabia since the birth of the Kingdom. The single Saudi royal family rules the millions of people in that oil-rich country, aided by the military support of the United States.

The people of Saudi Arabia are different than the Saudi government. Although the Saudi government is a close ally of the United States, the Saudi people are largely more hostile toward the United States than any other oil-rich country in the Arab Peninsula. It is partially for this reason that the United States' most tenacious foe (Osama bin Laden) and almost all of the hijackers who committed the 9/11 tragedy are from Saudi Arabia.

Let me share some of my stories when I was in Saudi Arabia. Saudi Arabia is one of the oil-richest and most oppressive countries in the world. The government prohibits political conversations, while members of the royal family are above the rule of law.

After Friday prayer in the afternoon, I would often see one or more Saudi or non-Saudi person convicted for drug-related and other different crimes being beheaded by the Saudi government in downtown Riyadh in front of thousands of people.

In the mid 1980s, I worked as a medical doctor in Sorrorah Medical Center in Riyadh Region. Prince Sultan bin Abdulaziz, who was the defense minister and brother of the ruling King Fahd, married an underage Saudi girl in the area where I was working as a medical doctor. The prince sultan divorced the young girl after several months. After the divorce, there was news circling among local people that Defense Minister Prince Sultan bin Abdulaziz did not want to have children from the young girl because she belonged to the Al-Badu Saudi tribes. The Al-Badu are Saudi people who are considered uncivilized because they usually live in the deserts of Saudi Arabia. Thus, the over sixty-year-old prince married the underage girl and then divorced her after several months just for immoral fun at the expense of a permanent stigma in the life of a young girl living in conservative Saudi society. This is only one example of numerous stories of the Saudi Royal family callousness that happened while I practiced medicine in the kingdom.

There was extreme limitation of free speech in Saudi Arabia. I worked in Saudi Arabia at different hospitals and health centers as a staff physician for almost eight years from 1983 to 1990. The kingdom was a very oppressive government that contained too many spies. I worked at Al-Nassim Medical

Center in Riyadh during the late 1980s. One day, I hazarded a simple joke about King Fahd in the presence of two persons. Twenty minutes later, a spy informed the Director of the Medical Center, whose name was Dr. Abdulrahman Fatani, about the joke. When I went to the director's office, he asked if I had told a joke about the king. I did not deny it. When I applied for the renewal of my medical contract at the end of that year with the Ministry of Health, the Saudi government refused to renew my contract. I went to the Director General of Health Affairs in Riyadh Region to determine the reason for the refusal. One of the top officials in the general director's office told me, in Arabic, "Aint thumzah alull kubar." ("You made fun of the big man.")

After eight years of working as a physician in the kingdom, I lost my job over a simple joke. If a simple joke can cost a job, how much more difficult would it be for Saudi people to overthrow the dictatorial and oppressive rule of the royal family in the hope of establishing democracy and freedom in the country? Ironically, because the US government has supported the Saudi regime for many, many years to keep its oil interests, if any democratic movement tried to change the oppressive Kingdom of Saudi Arabia into a democracy, the United States would be the first country to prevent that democracy and freedom in Saudi Arabia.

In 1983, I was looking for a job in Saudi Arabia. One day, I went to the headquarters of the Saudi National Guard in the city of Riyadh. I entered into a military general's office where I was supposed to meet the Saudi general about my job in a military hospital in Riyadh. The Saudi general was having a meeting with three US advisors and an English-Arabic interpreter. But when I saw the Saudi general with three US advisors and heard how they were speaking, the first thing that came to mind was the stark similarity between the

Soviet-occupied Afghanistan and US-supported Saudi Arabia. Advisors are advisors, whether from capitalist or communist countries.

I was in Saudi Arabia for eight years. The people of Saudi Arabia did not like the United States of America and considered it as the main cause of their oppression due to the US support of the royal family. Without the United States, the royal family could not rule the people of Saudi Arabia. Although the other oil-rich countries of Kuwait, Bahrain, Qatar, Oman, and the United Arab Emirates have been ruled by single families with the military support of the US and British governments, people in those countries are not as oppressed as the people in the Kingdom of Saudi Arabia. The ruling family in Saudi Arabia is extremely arrogant and harsh toward its people.

For this reason, there are thousands upon thousands of Saudi people who are thoroughly anti-American. It would be in the best interest of the United States to support democracy and freedom rather than an oppressive government ruled by a callous, single family in Saudi Arabia.

Democracy and the rule of majority would be more beneficial both for the United States and the Saudi people. To oppress and frustrate people is counterproductive and just increases violence and reactions. The more the oppression, the worse the reaction.

# CHAPTER 21:
# THE UNITED STATES AND TERRORISM

Terrorism is a political word. Most of the time combating, rival, opposing, and hostile parties accuse each other of terrorism. In 2008, during the United States presidential election vice-presidential candidate Sarah Palin accused Senator Barack Obama of links with domestic terrorism.

The United States often accuses Islamic religion of being supportive of terrorism, but in fact Islam is a religion of peace, mercy, kindness, and cooperation and the religion of the highest standards of morals and principles. Islamic religion not only prohibits terrorism—which is the use of murder, arson, kidnapping, and so forth to reach political objectives—but also prohibits all kind of killing, violence, brutality, oppression in its entirety whether political or not. Islam only allows Muslims to defend themselves against oppressors. Sadly—just like some Christian people who claim to follow a Prince of Peace and yet bomb medical clinics or practice horrific torture on people in jails—some people misinterpret Islam and think violence is acceptable.

Terrorism is almost the opposite of self-defense. Terrorism is illegal in many countries, but self-defense is legal almost universally. Certainly, all nations have the right to defend their sovereignty and liberty against foreign invaders and occupiers, but no nations have the right to be involved in terrorism. Terrorism should not be used against anyone, especially oppressed people, and oppressed people should not be labeled as terrorists for defending their sovereignty and liberty against foreign invaders.

The people of Afghanistan are hospitable, straightforward, and honest. They risk their own life to help others in need. There is no place for terrorism in the noble culture of the Afghan people. However, Afghan people have the legitimate right to defend their sovereignty and liberty against all foreign invaders; such defense is not terrorism.

I personally do not believe that political accusations of terrorism against any government, political party, or individual have any validity based on Article 11 of the Universal Declaration of Human Rights, "Everyone charged with a penal offense has the right to be presumed innocent until proved guilty according to law in a public trial at which he has had all the guarantees necessary for his defense." Terrorism, when used as rhetoric, is empty propaganda. But when it is the use of murder, arson, kidnapping, and so forth to reach political objectives, then it is an inhumane activity that should be condemned and defeated everywhere in the world.

Here are two stories of terrorism.

Many people in the United States may remember when an Egyptian passenger airplane Flight 990 left Kennedy International Airport on October 31, 1999 and suddenly plunged into the Atlantic, killing all 217 people onboard.

I was in Washington DC in 1999 and was engaged in conversation with a person a few months after the disaster. The person was a white American in his mid-thirties and was a physically strong man. During the conversation, he asked if I was Egyptian or Arab. I said I was neither, but was from Afghanistan. The person praised me and said that the Afghan people had done a good job of defeating the Soviet Union with the CIA's help.

He then asked if I had heard about Flight 990. I said that I'd heard about the accident from the media because it was a major disaster. The person told me that it was not an accident, but that the US had shot down the plane. I asked how this person knew and why the plane was shot down. He told me he was a federal employee of the US government. He confessed to me that he was one of the three federal employees who'd shot down the plane. The reason was because there were many Egyptian military officers onboard, and the US government did not want those military officers with higher military educations to go to Middle East, because it would endanger the security of Israel and US interests in the region. So it was not an accident that Flight 990 crashed.

Similarly, in December 1988, a bomb destroyed Pan American's Flight 103 over Lockerbie, Scotland killing all 243 passengers, 16 crewmembers, and 11 people on the ground. Approximately 180 of the dead were Americans, and the crash was one of the deadliest terrorist attacks against the United States to date. The US government accused the Libyan government of being responsible for the bomb. On May 29, 2002, Libya offered US$2.7 billion to settle the terrorism claims by the families of the 270 killed in the Lockerbie bombing.

Based on one of the perpetrators' voluntary confession, the United States could fulfill a similar moral and legal obligation if it treated the victims' families of Flight 990 in a similar manner.

The second story I would like to share with the readers happened in National City, California in the mid-2000s. I was speaking with a person and during the conversation the person told me quite abruptly that I looked like a good person to him. For that reason, he decided to tell me his story. He explained that life was too short and that he needed to share his story with at least one person before he died. He then told me that he was employed by the US federal government as a hit man. He then showed me a handgun under his jacket and a few foreign passports. He said that he never killed people in the US, but only assassinated politicians in Latin America. He said he had no relatives anywhere in world and didn't know who his biological parents were because people had raised him from childhood who were not his family. He described how a special plane would charter him to a particular country, drop him in a remote area or jungle, and pick him up again in the same plane after he'd assassinated his political target. He claimed to have more than forty passports, given to him by the US government whenever he went in-country. He told me how, if he died during the mission, no one would ever identify him or know who he was.

I asked how many people he'd killed. He claimed to have killed seventy-six politicians in South America so far. I asked about his name, and he said he had many and didn't even know what his real name was. He then assured me I would never see him again. He was a Spanish-American, approximately fifty years old. After hearing his story in National City, California, I was extremely distressed and disturbed. I told him to quit his job and do something else, because it was sinful and a crime against innocent people. He said he didn't care. The federal government paid him very well, and he had a good life.

One should remember also the terrorist tactics and over six hundred acts of terrorism annually that the US advisors recommended the Afghan mujahideen to commit during the Soviet-Afghan War in Afghanistan from 1982 through 1987.

In the present Afghan-American War, some Afghans now use those same military tactics against US forces and its allies that were taught to mujahideen by the CIA during the Soviet-Afghan War in 1980s.

I offered these two stories to inform the people about the facts and reality of terrorism and to help to eradicate worldwide terrorism and crimes against humanity.

# CHAPTER 22:
# THE CLEAR PATH TO GLOBAL PEACE

The main cause of the ongoing animosity and increasing violence in the world is neither global terrorism nor a global problem, but specific issues between the AAIA on one side and the Muslim world, Arab world, and radical Muslims on the other.

The global war on terrorism is political rhetoric launched by the AAIA to entice other countries to join them in solving their own self-created problems in the Islamic world.

Historically and presently, the AAIA is the most violent alliance of governments in the world. Currently, the AAIA are involved in four different wars against the Muslim world.

> The first war they are involved in fighting is against the entire Islamic world as a consequence of perpetuating since 1967 the occupation of the third holiest Islamic mosque of Al-Aqsa in East Jerusalem. As stated before, de-occupation of this mosque would mark the single-most effective gesture for reducing the hostility of the entire Muslim world toward the AAIA.

Allegations made by AAIA governments that Islam is intolerant to other cultures and religions, or opposed to democracy and the West are not true. Islam is a religion of peace, tolerance, and cooperation and reflects the highest morals and principles. Muslims are not against any other country in the world unless a country takes sides with AAIA policies that perpetuate this more than forty-year offense to all Muslims.

The hostility between the Islamic world and the AAIA will continue as long as the occupation of the Al-Aqsa Mosque persists. This is not because Islam issues threats, but because the AAIA policies, that permit this enormous offense to continue.

If the AAIA truly desired to live in peace with Muslims, they should simply end the occupation of the Al-Aqsa Mosque. If every day someone says, "I respect you" and they continue the same disrespectful behavior with you, you come to realize they are lying. One cannot want peace and desecrate another's holy shrine every day.

If Muslims occupied the Vatican in Rome, then Christians would feel the same spiritual pain that Muslims have felt for the past several decades by the occupation of Al-Aqsa Mosque by the AAIA. How can the Christian world be surprised by Islamic anger?

The AAIA cannot afford to confront the entire Islamic world forever. It would be better for them to respect Islam religion and liberate the Al-Aqsa Mosque. This would mark a tremendous step towards a sustainable global peace because it would lessen the anger of all Muslims and reduce a major recruiting point for extremist Islamic groups.

The liberation of the Al-Aqsa Mosque is not, and will never be, an issue only of Palestine or Arabs. It is a pan Islamic Issue.

> The second war is against the entire Arab world for the ongoing support and perpetuation of the Palestinian occupation since 1967. Again, the animosity of Arab people toward the AAIA will persist until the West Bank, Gaza and East Jerusalem are liberated as an independent Palestinian state side by side with Israel.

The United States and Great Britain will benefit politically and economically from establishing a Palestinian state because it would help to normalize relations with the people living in the other over twenty Arab countries of the world.

> The third war is fighting against Al-Qaeda, which is an Arab organization. If the United States and Great Britain want to eradicate the Al-Qaeda network, it will be necessary for them to promote genuine democracy in the oil-rich countries on the Arab Peninsula instead of supporting oppressive and dictatorial governments run by single families in Saudi Arabia, Kuwait, Bahrain, Qatar, Oman, and the United Arab Emirates.

Al-Qaeda is a product of oppression. The US and the British governments have militarily imposed the rule of single families at the expense of oppressing millions of people in the Arab Peninsula. I believe both governments will benefit from promoting democracy in the oil-rich countries of Saudi Arabia, Kuwait, Bahrain, Qatar, Oman, and the UAE, not only because it will reduce hostility toward them, but also because they will cease to appear as hypocrites who impose dictatorships on people in the name of democracy.

The fourth war is fighting the Afghan and Iraqi people. Occupied in 2001 and 2003, respectively, both nations were invaded based on now-disproven lies, which may have deceived people in the United States and Great Britain, but not elsewhere in the world. The rest of the world recognizes that the invasions were for the sake of access to petroleum resources.

When the lies were exposed, charges of terrorism were substituted. The Bush administration attempted the same move with Iran, but could not succeed in drumming up enough support to invade yet a third country on false pretenses.

The tens of thousands of US and the British troops in Iraq should have defeated all the anti-Anglo-American Arab fighters in their entirety. But those governments were not fighting primarily against Arab enemies—that is, for the sake of the security of the Iraqi people—but only for Iraq's oil. Had they been serious about defeating all Arab enemies, instead of begging the countries surrounding Iraq to prevent the flow of Arab fighters into Iraq, they should have welcomed those fighters, since they could then have been more easily dispatched and defeated. That way, the Anglo-American mission against terrorism would have been completed both in Iraq and in the region.

The Anglo-American allies occupied Afghanistan in 2001 on the claim that they wanted to either capture or kill Osama bin Laden in Afghanistan. But the media didn't mention the history that the US has with Osama bin Laden, or that the US had specifically requested he be sent to Afghanistan in the first place. After the Taliban was deposed, the United States and its allies then went on to kill tens of thousands of Afghan civilians, women, and children so far, but in eight years have yet to either kill or capture bin Laden. Benazir Bhutto, the assassinated former prime minister of Pakistan, has said publicly that bin Laden is already dead, yet the war in Afghanistan continues.

Even without such rumors, any sound mind should wonder how the capture or killing of just one person requires the presence of thousands and thousands of US and other forces in Afghanistan for over seven years. Stranger still, the US government has repeatedly said that Osama is not in Afghanistan, but lives in Pakistan. Why is Afghanistan, and not Pakistan, being invaded then?

In point of fact, the United States gives approximately seventy million dollars monthly in aid to Pakistan where Osama bin Laden is said to live. Pakistan has received nearly ten billion dollars so far during the US invasion of Afghanistan. Would Afghanistan receive such money if bin Laden actually lived in Afghanistan?

Afghan people are fighting for their freedom, their independence, and their sovereignty. Afghan people do not trust the AAIA for the reason that they are responsible for the bloodshed of Palestinian people for several decades now. Afghan people do not want Afghanistan to be a second Palestine.

I believe that contrary to the AAIA political rhetoric, the present hostility and violence in the world will not be eradicated by the global war on terrorism; rather, the opposite is true. The main reason for the global violence is the imperial greed of the AAIA that aims to control the political and economic life of other people in the world.

The joining of other countries with AAIA to fight against oppressed and occupied nations will not decrease the violence, but will further destabilize global peace and increase the violence.

To clarify again, Muslims are not simply against countries. Muslims are not against China, India, Japan, North Korea, South Korea, Switzerland, Russia, Germany, France, Venezuela, Cuba, Brazil, Mexico or any other country in the world, except when they involve themselves and help to perpetuate by further lies, misinformation, and terrorism the policies of the AAIA that keep the Al-Aqsa Mosque occupied by non-Muslims. So there is no reason to believe that Muslim people are otherwise against other countries in the world.

Similarly, the Arab world is not against any other country in the world, except AAIA and its supporters for the reason that no other country is occupying Palestine or involved in the killing of Palestinian-Arab people. So there is no reason to believe that Arab people are otherwise against other countries in the world.

To my knowledge, Al-Qaeda is not against other countries in the world, except AAIA and its supporters because they have not occupied Palestine and have not supported the ruling families in the oil-rich countries in the Arab peninsula.

The recent Mumbai tragedy in India in which hundreds of people were killed or injured was absolutely regional. The Islamic world is not against India, because India did not occupy the Al-Aqsa Mosque. And the Arab world is not against India, because India is not involved in the occupation or killing of Palestinian people. To my knowledge, Al-Qaeda is not against India, because India does not support the ruling, oppressive families in the oil-rich countries of the Arab peninsula. Kashmir's people triggered the Mumbai tragedy. The Kashmir's territorial issue has been a long-term problem between India and Pakistan. India and Pakistan have fought three wars so far over the Kashmir.

In order to decrease the ongoing, widespread hatred and violence in the world, I believe that it is absolutely necessary to address the fundamental reasons for the hostility between the AAIA and the Islamic world, the Arab world, and Al-Qaeda collectively. The political rhetoric of the global war on terror is a deception. It is absolutely not the true path to global peace.

The AAIA can definitely eradicate the violence and hostility in the world by taking specific steps to change its policies. Sadly, at present, it seems apparent that the AAIA do not want to achieve global peace because the stability and peace is contrary to AAIA interests in the world. Instability in oil-producing regions increases oil prices, for instance. Continuing to desecrate the Al-Aqsa Mosque guarantees that extremist Islamic parties will oppose that occupation, and thus create further pretexts for fighting Wars on Terror in order to occupy other countries. Wanting to have all money is the root of all evil. The greed of the AAIA serves only a tiny percentage of people in AAIA countries. Those people are not served by such greed; in fact, they are harmed, as citizens of those countries are now hated around the world and less safe. Because of greed, around the world the idea of democracy is now seen to be a hollow, ugly lie.

The AAIA has no other choice but the rhetoric of terrorism in order to continue the occupations of foreign countries and to take advantage of the oil resources in the world. But global peace should not be sacrificed just for the AAIA's interests in the world. The present war on terrorism is not a global issue, but is specifically limited to the AAIA.

Instead of being seduced by AAIA rhetoric, other countries in the world should come together to address the terrible consequences of the AAIA's agenda, which have made the entire world less safe. As one massive community, the world must resist the AAIA's greed, which continues to threaten global peace and the safety of hundreds of millions people in the world. Indeed, the AAIA together form the most powerful empire in the world, and it can be overwhelming and frightening, especially in isolation, to take on such an empire, but learn from Afghanistan, which remains undefeated by three of the world's most powerful empires to date. Collectively, empires can be defeated.

Full global peace cannot be achieved by joining the AAIA's effort to occupy and further oppress people in Afghanistan, Iraq, Palestine or any other countries in the world under the rhetoric of terrorism. Rather, by ending the occupations and ceasing the oppression of hundreds of millions of people in the Islamic world will bring world peace. More specifically, global peace can be achieved by:

The full liberation of the Al-Aqsa mosque in East Jerusalem. The full liberation of the Al-Aqsa Mosque will end the animosity between the Islamic world and the three anti-Islamic (AAIA) allies.

The full liberation of Palestine now occupied by the AAIA, and the restoration of an independent Palestinian State on the occupied Palestinian lands of the West Bank, Gaza and East Jerusalem side by side with Israel.

The withdrawal of US and British military forces from Afghanistan, Iraq, and the oil-rich countries of Saudi Arabia, Kuwait, Bahrain, Qatar, Oman, and the United Arab Emirates.

The promotion of democracy and democratically elected governments in the oil-rich countries of Saudi Arabia, Kuwait, Bahrain, Qatar, Oman, and the United Arab Emirates and other Arab countries, instead of ongoing support for dictatorial, single-family rule, which currently is a main cause for oppression and frustration for millions of people in the Middle East.

Anyone with a clear mind can see that the first item could be done virtually overnight. Without a doubt, simply to do the first task would increase global peace virtually overnight. It is the easiest step to take, and probably the most profoundly effective one. The AAIA can do the second item in a matter of weeks. They are not difficult tasks, if only the AAIA would cease to be merely stubborn in its bigotry against the people occupied. The third item could be done in a matter of months. However, it is unlikely that the AAIA will accomplish these simple steps in order to achieve global peace, because the AAIA have tremendous interest in these four wars against the Islamic world. As a matter of fact, both creation and continuation of wars are an integral part of the Anglo-American-Israeli policy; because the influential weapon producing industries in those countries make tremendous profit from war. It is called the War Complex. There are currently more than ten million refugees in the world, almost five million are displaced by the Anglo-American-Israeli allies (The Axis of Oppression).

I hope it happens soon for the sake of global peace and the peace of all people in AAIA and non-AAIA countries alike.

# CHAPTER 23:
# THE US CLAIMS FOR HUMAN RIGHTS AND EQUAL OPPORTUNITY

Before addressing the issues of human rights and equal opportunity, it is necessary to mention some relevant facts.

I came to the United States in the early 1990s. I was watching and listening to US media with interest because I'd heard that the United States was a free society. I assumed that what the US media was telling to the American people were true. But I realized very soon that the US media was just as political and biased as the US government, and did not tell true stories and facts to the American people when it came to certain things.

I have been very familiar with political, economical and social conditions in Afghanistan. Almost all of the news I have heard about Afghanistan was either fabricated or fatally biased. What was reported flatly contradicted with the facts and reality on the ground.

I knew some employees working in Voice of America (VOA) in Washington DC, which broadcasts programs that are regularly listened to in Afghanistan. At the very beginning in 2002, I requested an interview to speak about Hamid Karzai and his Northern Alliance government in Kabul on the subject its incompetence to rule the country and that it would fail in its entirety, but VOA rejected my request. One of the employees at VOA explained to me that they are a branch of the State Department of the United States. The VOA should justify US foreign policy and would never be able to make an interview about the inherent flaws of the Karzai government because such an interview would question and contradict US policy in Afghanistan. The employee said that such an interview would have consequences for the VOA employees, because they are regularly instructed by the State Department that all broadcasts are meant to justify US foreign policies in the world.

In 2002, my interview was not intended to be against anyone in particular, but only to clarify the fact that the longer Karzai and his Northern Alliance warlords stay in power, the worse the situation will become in Afghanistan, which has proven to be the case now in 2009. The US pro-American Karzai government has failed after seven years, despite the fact that the United States and its allies have killed tens of thousands of Afghan people and have spent billions of dollars in military expenses in Afghanistan.

Afghan people would have made a better and more successful government than the Karzai and Northern Alliance government in Afghanistan. I have sent many letters to US administrations explaining the clear path to peace that will prevent the foreseeable and future violence and bloodshed in Afghanistan, but the administration was as arrogant as its military. The Karzai government installed by the Bush administration was neither wanted nor desired by the Afghan people, but it was imposed nevertheless in Afghanistan. For this reason, the pro-

American Karzai government made by the United States has failed after seven years in its entirety.

The United States government cannot sell the real reasons for its actions to Americans— because the US government serves the interests of a very small extremely rich minority of Americans—and so US administrations have no choice but to exaggerate and deceive the American public in order to pursue specific economic and political interests in the world. The most notorious instance of this is the now wholly discredited weapons of mass destruction argument used as a pretext to invade Iraq for its oil. The AAIA allies all have weapons of mass destruction (WMD), and the United States has been so far, the first country in the world which has ever used nuclear weapons to kill 220,000 Japanese, mostly civilian. Israel has atomic weapons without being signatories to the Nuclear Non-Proliferation Act that almost all countries have had to sign. Since clearly some countries are allowed to have such weapons. In 1960 the CIA determined that the Israeli nuclear weapons program was an established and irreversible fact. In 1998, the US estimated that Israel possesses 200 nuclear weapons. The Dimona Nuclear Reactor is an established WMD producing facility in Israel. The USA and UK justify Israel's WMD and claim that the Israel has the right to possess weapons of mass destruction for self defense. On the contrary, the USA and UK argue that other countries such as the Islamic Republic of Iran should not have access to nuclear tecnology. For peace and stability, all countries in the region including the Zionist regime of Israel should not be allowed to have access to WMD. The AAIA's outcries about Iran's nuclear technology are biased and pure nonsense on the ground that Iran needs nuclear technology more than Israel in order to defend itself against the AAIA aggression. The Islamic Republic of Iran is surrendered by tens of thousands of American and British troops currently in Iraq and Afghanistan which directly threat the oil-rich Iran national security. The AAIA aggressive policy toward the Islamic world prompted many countries including Iran to develop nuclear technology in order to be secured from the AAIA aggression. All countries which are in the possession of WMD could defend themselves and are secured from the AAIA invasion. If Iraq had had WMD, the USA and UK would never have invaded Iraq. The USA and UK invaded the oil-rich Iraq because they were well aware of the fact before the invasion in 2003 that there were no WMD in Iraq. The International Atomic Energy Agency (IAEA) had completed its intensive search for WMD in Iraq before the invasion, but WMD were not found. North Korea has WMD and can defend itself, for this reason the United States is trying to avoid arm confrontation with the nuclear-armed North Korea. United States can not invade the nuclear-armed Pakistan where Osama bin Laden lives; because Pakistan has WMD and can defend itself against foreign invasion. In addition, the USA gives tens of millions of dollars every month to Pakistan in order to buy its support in the current Afghan-American war.

The United States and its allies believe that they have the right to possess of weapons of mass destruction and have the right to use them as was shown in Japan, but do not want other countries have the same privileges. In fact all human beings are equal in dignity and rights.

The Iraq invasion shows clearly how, in the United States political system, the majority of American people are the victims of the interest of the small percentage of the richest Americans. The oil companies made records profits. Exxon Mobile made 45.2 billion dollars in 2008 at the expense of more than 4,000 Americans killed and more than 30,000 Americans injured or permanently disabled since the war began in 2003. The cost to US tax payers for the war in Iraq reached around three billion dollars per week for several years.

The United States claims of "equal opportunity", and "equal prosperity" contradict the reality on the ground. Like most countries, whatever their politics, a very small minority of extremely rich individuals own the bulk of the wealth in America. And with respect to the whole world, the US represents the very small minority of wealth-holding individuals.

Professor Edward Wolff stated in an interview in May 2003 that the United States is more unequal than any other advanced industrial country. Mr. Wolff said that the top 5 percent had more wealth than the remaining 95 percent of the population, collectively. He said that the bottom 20 percent have zero wealth. They either have no assets, or their debt equals or exceeds their assets

Edward Wolff is a professor of economics at New York University. He is the author of many books on economic and tax policy and is managing editor of the *Review of Income and Wealth*.

This extreme inequality and economic injustice are bad for humanity and have disastrous consequences for the bottom 90 percent of American people and the world at large.

According to UNICEF's report, thirty thousand children die every day due to poverty—ten million annually.[6]

One in every fifty children is homeless in the United States—or 1.5 million total.

---

6     See Black, R. E., Morris, S. S., and Bryce, J. (28 June 2003). "Where and why are 10 million children dying every year?" *The Lancet*, 361(9376), pp. 2226-2234.

The US political and social system deceives the bottom 90 percent Americans with ideas of equal opportunity and equal prosperity and are purposely keeps them unaware of the full extent of unjust wealth distribution. Because the US government protects the interests of a very small wealthy minority of Americans, 90 percent of the American people suffer. In the US political and economic system, the richest become richer and the poor become poorer. There are over three million Americans who are homeless and do not have basic needs like houses, showers, or decent food, and their numbers are increasing steadily. In the United States, over forty-five million Americans do not have health insurance, which is now a necessity to live, at least in industrialized nations where the number of toxins in food, water and the air has increased exponentially in the last thirty years. Based on a recent study, nearly half of all Americans want to live elsewhere in the world.

I have been living in San Diego, California for the past seventeen years. I have never seen a single homeless cat or dog. These pets live in very beautiful houses and apartment buildings, but there are thousands of American people on the streets without homes and basic needs. Those homeless Americans are citizens of the United States and deserve a better life and care, but are ignored by an unkind and unjust system in the United States. These desperate homeless Americans are the victims of the extreme social and economic injustice in the United States' system. Extreme inequality is bad for humanity.

In the United States, the prosperity of 90 percent of the American people is sacrificed for a very small wealthy minority in the United States. The US claim of equal opportunity and equal prosperity is untrue.

In the same way, allegations of human rights violation against other governments are largely political rhetoric for the reason that the human rights abused by the AAIA are greater and more serious than their adversaries. It would be better for the AAIA to see its past and present history of human rights abuses in the mirror of human rights and then compare themselves with those who are being accused around the world.

As a historic fact the British Empire occupied one quarter of the world and oppressed almost one quarter of the entire world's population for decades. The British government occupied America, Canada, Australia, and New Zealand and exploited them all primarily for their own benefit. The British killed or subdued the native people of America, Canada, Australia, and New Zealand and permanently took away these countries from the native people. For instance, the remnants of the Native Americans in the United States live in the remote areas in Indian reservations in deserts out side the cities in their own homeland. This continues to the present day. It is not an "offense" limited only to the historical past.

Although the United States, Canada, Australia, New Zealand are different countries, they are now dominated by the same ethnically English descendants who left their small British Isles and took over these countries from the native people. In the present time, Queen Elizabeth who is not only the queen of the United Kingdom, but also the Queen of Canada, Australia and New Zealand.

In addition, the British Empire was complicit in the creation of the Israeli State on Palestinian land by the help of the United States of America in 1947.

The British along with other European partners were involved in the trans-Atlantic transportations of hundreds of thousands innocent human beings from Africa to America from the seventeenth century forward for exploitation and slavery, which is considered one the most inhuman acts imaginable. As just one illustration, human beings who became ill during transportation were thrown from the ships to drown. The slavery in British North America started around 1619 and continued for almost 240 years until the proclamation issued by President Abraham Lincoln on January 1, 1863 that declared all slaves were free.

Although discrimination is unlawful according to the United States Constitution, in fact this is often only of symbolic importance because there still is ongoing and massive systemic discrimination against African-Americans, Muslims, and other minorities in the United States.

In order to distract the attention of the world people from the human rights abuses both from their past and in the present, the United States and British established and funded the Human Rights Watch Organization.

This organization purports to be independent, but in fact it is biased, hired and funded by the United States and its allies to politically serve their interests. The Human Rights Watch Organization has only two functions. First, to distract the world about the human rights abuses committed by the AAIA, and second, to make propaganda and accusations that damage the credibility of governments, groups, or individuals that the AAIA labels as adversaries around the world.

For instance, in the present Afghan-American War, the Human Rights Watch Organization in Kabul is not reporting on the massive human rights violations by the US and its allies in Afghanistan. The US government is using dogs to kill Afghan people inside their homes based on mere speculation. Recently in 2009, in one instance in Khoost province in Afghanistan, the US army's dogs entered a civilian Afghan's house and attacked and killed an entire Afghan family, including women and children. There are numerous similar cases, but I cited just this one because I personally know a member of the victims' family. He is a pharmacist and graduated from Kabul University. Meanwhile, the Human Rights Watch Organization office in Kabul turns a blind eye to such attacks, and does not report them to the world.

According to the Universal Declaration of Human Rights, everyone charged with a penal offense has the right to be presumed innocent until proved guilty according to law in a public trial at which he or she has had all the guarantees necessary for his defense. On the contrary, in one well-documented case in Northern Afghanistan, the US and its allies forces killed and collectively burned 2,000 captured Afghans to death during the invasion in 2001.

By contrast, in the ongoing Afghan-American War, the US military uses animals to kill innocent civilians, including women and children, without any benefit of legal proceedings. They are executed without a trial, often without even charges ever being leveled against them—nothing but rumors or allegations.

Elsewhere in the world, for three weeks Israel terrorized one and a half million Palestinians in the besieged prison of Gaza strip with bombardment from the ground, sea and air, which massacred thousands civilian women and children with the help of the military and political support from the United States. At least when the Nazis practiced genocide, the United States intervened to stop them—why not in Palestine?

Many governments in the world—not only the AAIA governments—have elections and democracy based on written constitutions and laws made by representatives elected by people.

Civilization does not accept extreme inequality and economic injustice, abandoning tens of thousands of mentally and physically disabled human beings to live on the streets without housing and other basic needs, the biting and killing of civilian women and children by dogs, the occupation and the killing of innocent people in their own countries just to steal their wealth, the use of violence and heavy-handed military tactics against defenseless people, discrimination against minorities, oppression and tyranny against religious freedom, or the fabrication of misleading propaganda in order to deceive the public—and yet, these are all integral to the AAIA's agenda and policies.

For the safety and prosperity of the majority of American, British and Israeli people the AAIA governments should not destroy the world-image of equal opportunity, human rights, peace, morals, and civilization by using them as slogans of political rhetoric to deceive their own people and the world at large. The AAIA is key to the global peace and prosperity as these three allies affect not only the life of their own people, but also the lives of hundreds of millions of other people in the world.

Many readers might not have had the chance to read the Universal Declaration of Human Rights. I offer it below so readers may judge for themselves if the actions of the countries they live in are in accord with, or are in violation, of this Declaration. It should be noted that any violation of the thirty Articles contained in the Universal Deceleration of Human Rights is considered an abuse of universal human rights; that is, rights that are held in common by all people and cannot be denied to anyone under any circumstances.

# THE UNIVERSAL DECLARATION OF HUMAN RIGHTS

On December 10, 1948, the General Assembly of the United Nations adopted and proclaimed the Universal Declaration of Human Rights, the full text of which appears in the following pages. Following this historic act, the Assembly called upon all member countries to publicize the text of the Declaration and "to cause it to be disseminated, displayed, read and expounded principally in schools and other educational institutions, without distinction based on the political status of countries or territories." To date, this task has not been accomplished in the United States.

PREAMBLE

Whereas recognition of the inherent dignity and of the equal and inalienable rights of all members of the human family is the foundation of freedom, justice and peace in the world,

Whereas disregard and contempt for human rights have resulted in barbarous acts which have outraged the conscience of mankind, and the advent of a world in which human beings shall enjoy freedom of speech and belief and freedom from fear and want has been proclaimed as the highest aspiration of the common people,

Whereas it is essential, if man is not to be compelled to have recourse, as a last resort, to rebellion against tyranny and oppression, that human rights should be protected by the rule of law,

Whereas it is essential to promote the development of friendly relations between nations,
Whereas the peoples of the United Nations have in the Charter reaffirmed their faith in fundamental human rights, in the dignity and worth of the human person and in the equal rights of men and women and have determined to promote social progress and better standards of life in larger freedom,

Whereas Member States have pledged themselves to achieve, in co-operation with the United Nations, the promotion of universal respect for and observance of human rights and fundamental freedoms,

Whereas a common understanding of these rights and freedoms is of the greatest importance for the full realization of this pledge,

**Now, Therefore THE GENERAL ASSEMBLY proclaims THIS UNIVERSAL DECLARATION OF HUMAN RIGHTS** as a common standard of achievement for all peoples and all nations, to the end that every individual and every organ of society, keeping this Declaration constantly in mind, shall strive by teaching and education to promote respect for these rights and freedoms and by progressive measures, national and international, to secure their universal and effective recognition and observance, both among the peoples of Member States themselves and among the peoples of territories under their jurisdiction.

### Article 1.

All human beings are born free and equal in dignity and rights. They are endowed with reason and conscience and should act towards one another in a spirit of brotherhood.

### Article 2.

Everyone is entitled to all the rights and freedoms set forth in this Declaration, without distinction of any kind, such as race, colour, sex, language, religion, political or other opinion, national or social origin, property, birth or other status. Furthermore, no distinction shall be made on the basis of the political, jurisdictional or international status of the country or territory to which a person belongs, whether it be independent, trust, non-self-governing or under any other limitation of sovereignty.

### Article 3.

Everyone has the right to life, liberty and security of person.

### Article 4.

No one shall be held in slavery or servitude; slavery and the slave trade shall be prohibited in all their forms.

### Article 5.

No one shall be subjected to torture or to cruel, inhuman or degrading treatment or punishment.

**Article 6.**

Everyone has the right to recognition everywhere as a person before the law.

**Article 7.**

All are equal before the law and are entitled without any discrimination to equal protection of the law. All are entitled to equal protection against any discrimination in violation of this Declaration and against any incitement to such discrimination.

**Article 8.**

Everyone has the right to an effective remedy by the competent national tribunals for acts violating the fundamental rights granted him by the constitution or by law.

**Article 9.**

No one shall be subjected to arbitrary arrest, detention or exile.

**Article 10.**

Everyone is entitled in full equality to a fair and public hearing by an independent and impartial tribunal, in the determination of his rights and obligations and of any criminal charge against him.

**Article 11.**

(1) Everyone charged with a penal offence has the right to be presumed innocent until proved guilty according to law in a public trial at which he has had all the guarantees necessary for his defense.

(2) No one shall be held guilty of any penal offence on account of any act or omission which did not constitute a penal offence, under national or

international law, at the time when it was committed. Nor shall a heavier penalty be imposed than the one that was applicable at the time the penal offence was committed.

## Article 12.

No one shall be subjected to arbitrary interference with his privacy, family, home or correspondence, nor to attacks upon his honor and reputation. Everyone has the right to the protection of the law against such interference or attacks.

## Article 13.

(1) Everyone has the right to freedom of movement and residence within the borders of each state.

(2) Everyone has the right to leave any country, including his own, and to return to his country.

## Article 14.

(1) Everyone has the right to seek and to enjoy in other countries asylum from persecution.

(2) This right may not be invoked in the case of prosecutions genuinely arising from non-political crimes or from acts contrary to the purposes and principles of the United Nations.

## Article 15.

(1) Everyone has the right to a nationality.

(2) No one shall be arbitrarily deprived of his nationality nor denied the right to change his nationality.

## Article 16.

(1) Men and women of full age, without any limitation due to race, nationality or religion, have the right to

marry and to found a family. They are entitled to equal rights as to marriage, during marriage and at its dissolution.

(2) Marriage shall be entered into only with the free and full consent of the intending spouses.

(3) The family is the natural and fundamental group unit of society and is entitled to protection by society and the State.

### Article 17.

(1) Everyone has the right to own property alone as well as in association with others.

(2) No one shall be arbitrarily deprived of his property.

### Article 18.

Everyone has the right to freedom of thought, conscience and religion; this right includes freedom to change his religion or belief, and freedom, either alone or in community with others and in public or private, to manifest his religion or belief in teaching, practice, worship and observance.

### Article 19.

Everyone has the right to freedom of opinion and expression; this right includes freedom to hold opinions without interference and to seek, receive and impart information and ideas through any media and regardless of frontiers.

### Article 20.

(1) Everyone has the right to freedom of peaceful assembly and association.

(2) No one may be compelled to belong to an association.

**Article 21.**

(1) Everyone has the right to take part in the government of his country, directly or through freely chosen representatives.

(2) Everyone has the right of equal access to public service in his country.

(3) The will of the people shall be the basis of the authority of government; this shall be expressed in periodic and genuine elections which shall be by universal and equal suffrage and shall be held by secret vote or by equivalent free voting procedures.

**Article 22.**

Everyone, as a member of society, has the right to social security and is entitled to realization, through national effort and international co-operation and in accordance with the organization and resources of each State, of the economic, social and cultural rights indispensable for his dignity and the free development of his personality.

**Article 23.**

(1) Everyone has the right to work, to free choice of employment, to just and favorable conditions of work and to protection against unemployment.

(2) Everyone, without any discrimination, has the right to equal pay for equal work.

(3) Everyone who works has the right to just and favorable remuneration ensuring for himself and his family an existence worthy of human dignity, and supplemented, if necessary, by other means of social protection.

(4) Everyone has the right to form and to join trade unions for the protection of his interests.

**Article 24.**

Everyone has the right to rest and leisure, including reasonable limitation of working hours and periodic holidays with pay.

**Article 25.**

(1) Everyone has the right to a standard of living adequate for the health and well-being of himself and of his family, including food, clothing, housing and medical care and necessary social services, and the right to security in the event of unemployment, sickness, disability, widowhood, old age or other lack of livelihood in circumstances beyond his control.

(2) Motherhood and childhood are entitled to special care and assistance. All children, whether born in or out of wedlock, shall enjoy the same social protection.

**Article 26.**

(1) Everyone has the right to education. Education shall be free, at least in the elementary and fundamental stages. Elementary education shall be compulsory. Technical and professional education shall be made generally available and higher education shall be equally accessible to all on the basis of merit.

(2) Education shall be directed to the full development of the human personality and to the strengthening of respect for human rights and fundamental freedoms. It shall promote understanding, tolerance and friendship among all nations, racial or religious groups, and shall further the activities of the United Nations for the maintenance of peace.

(3) Parents have a prior right to choose the kind of education that shall be given to their children.

**Article 27.**

(1) Everyone has the right freely to participate in the cultural life of the community, to enjoy the arts and to share in scientific advancement and its benefits.

(2) Everyone has the right to the protection of the moral and material interests resulting from any scientific, literary or artistic production of which he is the author.

**Article 28.**

Everyone is entitled to a social and international order in which the rights and freedoms set forth in this Declaration can be fully realized.

**Article 29.**

(1) Everyone has duties to the community in which alone the free and full development of his personality is possible.

(2) In the exercise of his rights and freedoms, everyone shall be subject only to such limitations as are determined by law solely for the purpose of securing due recognition and respect for the rights and freedoms of others and of meeting the just requirements of morality, public order and the general welfare in a democratic society.

(3) These rights and freedoms may in no case be exercised contrary to the purposes and principles of the United Nations.

**Article 30.**

Nothing in this Declaration may be interpreted as implying for any State, group or person any right to engage in any activity or to perform any act aimed at the destruction of any of the rights and freedoms set forth herein.

# CHAPTER 24:
# THE BRITISH EMPIRE OCCUPIED ONE QUARTER OF THE WORLD, BUT NEVER SUCCEDED IN OCCUPYING AFGHANISTAN

The British Empire was the largest empire in the history and, for over a century, was a global superpower. It began in the fifteenth century. At the peak of its power, it was said that "the sun never sets on the British Empire" because its span across the globe ensured that the sun was always shining on at least one of its numerous colonies.

In 1914, the British empire occupied one quarter of the world, or more than fifty countries, including: Ireland, Canada, Egypt, Yemen, Oman, Bahrain, UAE, India, the area of what is now Pakistan, Iraq, Sri Lanka, Burma, Bhutan, Nepal, Bangladesh, the Maldives, the Seychelles, Mauritius, Andaman Islands, Malaya, Malaysia, Singapore, Brunei, a few small parts of China, Australia, New Zealand, Palestine, Papua New Guinea, Vanuatu, Solomon Islands, Fiji, Tonga, Sudan,

Somalia, Gambia, Sierra Leone, Ghana, Nigeria, Kenya, Uganda, Tanzania, Lesotho, Botswana, Zimbabwe, South Africa, Swaziland, Zambia, Malawi, Namibia, Bermuda, Guyana, Belize, the Cayman Islands, and the West Indies. The British Empire occupied all these countries in order to exploit the economic and political lives of more than one quarter of the world's population.

The following is a history of the British invasions of Afghanistan. This information was presented earlier, in a different context, but there are some additions here that further amplify the issue. This history bears on the question of terrorism and global peace because it illustrates how the greatest empire in the world history after the Roman over a period of decades was unable to successfully occupy Afghanistan. This is not simply Afghan pride, but would have served as a warning to the Soviets before their ill-advised adventure in Afghanistan, and still serves as a warning to the US and its allies, if only they would heed it.

During the nineteenth century, Afghanistan was invaded by British India with the intention of limiting Russian influence. There was ongoing struggle in Asia between the British Empire and Russia. The British claimed that Afghanistan could become a route for Russia to invade British India. The British's ambition to occupy Afghanistan resulted in three Anglo-Afghan wars.

The First Anglo-Afghan War between British and Afghan forces occurred from 1838 to 1842. The governor general of British India, Lord Auckland, ordered the invasion of Afghanistan in 1838 with the object of restoring Shah Shuja to power. Shah Shuja had had close relations with the British Empire in India. Shah Shuja had already ruled Afghanistan from 1803 to 1809 before being deposed, in part for being too pro-British.

The British army first invaded Afghanistan from Punjab in British India to occupy the country, and then invaded Kandahar and Ghazni. In August 1839, Shah Shuja was enthroned for the second time in Kabul by the British's support after almost thirty years.

The British claimed that they did not want to occupy Afghanistan but only wanted to restore Shah Shuja's government in Kabul. This trick fooled no one.

Omens of disaster for the British abounded. Opposition to Shah Shuja began as soon as he assumed the throne; soon, the power of his government did not extend beyond the areas controlled by the invading forces of British India.

The Afghans resented the British presence and Shah Shuja's government. As the occupation dragged on, Sir William MacNaghten allowed his soldiers to bring in their families to improve morale. This further infuriated the Afghans, as it appeared that the British were settling into a permanent occupation.

Wazeer Muhammad Akbar Khan was the top commander of the Afghan forces fighting against the British forces at the time. In November 1841, Afghan forces in Kabul killed senior British officer Sir Alexander Burnes and his aides. In the following weeks, the British commanders tried to negotiate with Wazeer Mohammad Akbar Khan. In a secret meeting, Sir William MacNaghten, one of the principal architects of the invasion of Afghanistan, tried first to bribe Wazeer Mohammad Akbar Khan in exchange for allowing the British to stay. Rather than betray his countrymen, Wazeer Mohammad Akbar Khan ordered MacNaghten to be thrown in prison. Along the way to prison, the Afghan warriors killed MacNaghten and his dismembered corpse was paraded through Kabul.

On January 1, 1842, the British's retreat began. The army at that time was composed of approximately 16,500 troops.

On January 6–13, 1842, in the Gandamak Battle, Wazeer Mohammad Akbar Khan's Afghan forces defeated the British army. Gandamak is a place between Kabul and Jalalabad in Afghanistan. Wazeer Mohammad Akbar Khan was declared a hero.

As the British forces struggled to retreat to Jalalabad, the British were attacked by Ghilzai Pashtun warriors. The retreating British army was completely massacred with one exception. Dr. William Brydon was allowed to escape, and arrived at the gates of Jalalabad to tell of the British defeat.

Shah Shuja remained in power only a few months after his British protectors were gone before he was assassinated in April 1842. Ironically, both Shah Shuja and the current puppet-president Hamid Karzai belong to the same tribe in Afghanistan.

From 1878 to1880, the British invaded Afghanistan for a second time, and again failed to occupy Afghanistan. On July 27, 1880, the British army was defeated by the Afghan fighters led by Ayub Khan in the battle of Maiwand in Kandahar. In the battle of Maiwand, the greatest Afghan heroine and the unforgettable Afghan lady Malai played an important and glorious role. She is still remembered to this day for her sacrifice of being shot dead by the British troops during the Maiwand battle.

The Third Anglo-Afghan War occurred in 1919, when the Afghanistan's King Amir Amanullah Khan rejected British control of his foreign policy and declared Afghanistan fully independent. King Amanullah Khan eventually secured the full independence of Afghanistan through the Treaty of Rawalpindi in 1919 after a month-long war.

With the liberation of Afghanistan from Britain, Amanullah Khan became a national hero and turned his attention to reforming and modernizing his country. King Amanullah was ethnically Pashtun Afghan and was one of the most popular and admired rulers in Afghan history.

During the three Anglo-Afghan wars, the British committed numerous atrocities in Afghanistan. Over twenty thousand British Indian troops were killed. Exact Afghan casualties are still unknown, but it is estimated the Afghan causalities were higher given the weapon superiority enjoyed by the British army. That superiority did not help them win, however— another cautionary note for the US, with its impressively advanced modern weaponry in Afghanistan.

The British invaded Afghanistan three times, but never succeeded in occupying Afghanistan even though at its peak in 1914 it occupied fifty countries over one quarter of the world.

Most British colonies were liberated from British rule after World War II in 1945 because the British Empire collapsed and became too weak to rule the occupied countries.

One of the obvious differences between the British and other colonizing powers—like France, Spain, Italy, or Portugal— was that the British Empire left long-term problems in their colonized countries, which now are the fundamental causes of present violence and bloodshed in many places in the world.

For instance, the British were involved in the creation of Kashmir's current issue between India and Pakistan in 1947 during the partition of India. Kashmir is a predominantly Muslim province, but the majority part of Kashmir is under the Indian rule. The Kashmir's issue has incited three wars between Pakistan and India with tens of thousands of people killed. The Kashmir issue is still not resolved and is the main reason for violence and hatred between Pakistan and India, the two nuclear rivals in the region.

Kuwait was one of the provinces of Iraq, but the British separated the oil-rich province of Kuwait from Iraq, and made it a separate government. The Kuwait issue partially incited Iraq's invasion of Kuwait in 1990.

The British government was involved in the creation of Israel in Palestine, which is now the most difficult problem between Arabs and Israelis, and has been the fundamental cause of bloodshed between Arabs and Israelis for several decades.

Britain was involved in the creation of the apartheid regime in South Africa, which resulted in racial hatred among its people and caused thousands of deaths in that country.

Afghan people defeated the British Empire in three Anglo-Afghan wars. Later, the British created the border problem of the so-called Durand's Line between Afghanistan and British India. Currently, Durand's Line divides Afghanistan and Pakistan in the southeast, and separates the sole Pashtun ethnicity on both sides of that borderline. Durand's line represents a retaliatory division of the Pashtun majority by the British.

Dispute over the Durand Line began with its creation by British Empire in 1893. At that time Afghanistan was ruled by Amir Abdulrahman Khan the so-called Iron Amir. This division continues to the present day. Thus, the ongoing violence on the southeast side of the Durand's Line that US, its allies, and Pakistani forces have all failed to quell in the Pashtun tribal areas is a direct result of the British Empire's conspiracy.

In conclusion, much of the ongoing bloodshed, hatred and suffering of millions of people in the world is a consequence of the British-made problems, including the Israel and Palestine, the Kashmir, Durand's Line, the Iraq and Kuwait, the South African apartheid, and so forth. Much of this misery is a result of failed adventurism by the British Empire. In the short term, they selfishly exploited local resources, and then irresponsibly fled when those interests changed, or when they could no longer enforce their rule.

Hopefully those who, now or in the future, believe that they can defeat and occupy Afghanistan will heed the example of this failure.

# CHAPTER 25:
# THE KOH-I-NOOR DIAMOND
# IN THE TOWER OF LONDON

As a historic fact, the British Empire took the Koh-i-Noor diamond from Afghanistan during the first British-Afghan War. The diamond is now housed in the Tower of London.

The true story of the diamond is as follows:

Found in India some four millennia ago, the Koh-i-Noor diamond is the oldest recorded diamond in the world. It is priceless. Originally, it weighed 186 carats and was an oval stone but was later re-cut to 108.93 carats.

Eventually, the diamond came into the possession of the Mughal emperors in India. It was set in the famous Peacock Throne of the Mughal Emperor Shah Jehan as one of the peacock's eyes. Shah Jehan was a Muslim Emperor who is famous for building the historic Taj Mahal complex in memory of his wife Queen Mumtaz Mahal at Agra, India. The Taj is considered the most beautiful monument built by the Muslim rulers of India. It is regarded as one of the eight wonders of the world, and some Western historians have noted that its architectural beauty has never been surpassed.

In 1738, Nadir Shah Afshar (the Persian Napoleon) invaded the Afghan territory and marched on to India. Nadir defeated the Mughal army at the huge Battle of Karnal in February 1739. Nadir then captured the Mughal emperor Mohammad Shah and entered with him into Delhi. Mohammad Shah ransomed himself by handing over the keys to his royal treasury, thereby losing even the Peacock Throne to the Persian emperor. Nadir Shah took the diamond and named it "Koh-i-Noor" (or "Mountain of Light" in Farsi). The Persian troops left Delhi in 1739, and brought the Koh-i-Noor diamond to Persia.

Nadir Shah Afshar had secured control of most of Afghanistan and part of India. He adopted a stance of reconciliation towards the Afghans because he wisely understood that he could not afford an indefinite rivalry with them. In the Persian army of Nadir Shah Afshar, there was a Pashtun Afghan military officer named Ahmad Shad Durrani. Nadir believed that the Pashtun Afghans were superior warriors.

According to Afghan history, it is said that Nadir Shah Afshar summoned Ahmad Shah Durrani to Delhi and said, "After me, the kingship will pass on to you."

After the assassination of Nadir Shah Afshar in 1747, his empire fell into chaos. Ahmad Shah Durrani became the Amir of Khorasan and founded an independent Afghanistan in his region in 1747. Thus, the Koh-i-Noor diamond fell into the possession of Ahmad Shah Durrani.

Later, when the pro-British King Shah Shuja was deposed in 1809, he escaped to British India with the Koh-i-Noor diamond. The British imprisoned him in India and forced him to hand over the Koh-i-Noor Diamond to the governor of the Punjab province in British India Maharajah Ranjit Singh.

The British sought to justify this tacit theft of the Koh-i-Noor diamond with the coercive Treaty of Lahore on March 29, 1849, which stated, "The gem called the Koh-i-Noor which was taken from Shah Shuja-ul-Mulk by Maharajah Ranjit Singh shall be surrendered by the Maharajah of Lahore to the Queen of England."

Soon after, the British sent the diamond to England. The Koh-i-Noor left the shores of India on April 6, 1850. Upon reaching London on July 2, 1850, it was handed to Queen Victoria. The queen was jubilant when she received the stolen Koh-i-Noor diamond and recorded in her journal, "The jewels are truly magnificent. I am very happy that the British Crown will possess these jewels for I shall certainly make them Crown Jewels." It has since been worn by England's Queen Alexandra, Queen Mary, and, in 1937, was worn by Queen Elizabeth for her coronation. Presently, the diamond is in the Tower of London.

It is unpleasantly ironic that the British are once again invading Afghanistan with an intent to further rob that country of its treasures—this time oil and natural gas. Just as the problems and wreckage of past British adventurism have left scars all over the world, what makes them particularly offensive to Afghan people is not only the fact of these crimes, but even more so the denial of them. The Afghan people are straightforward and honest—the denial of wrongdoing is a great offense in Afghan culture. And yet, even at this moment, the people of Israel and Palestine, the people of Iraq and Kuwait, the Pashtun Afghans separated by the Durand Line, and the people of the Kashmir—only to name a few—continue to experience repercussions from British irresponsibility with no acknowledgement or reparations or even a simple apology for their actions. Instead—they have invaded Afghanistan for a fourth time with their US allies, not only compounding their past wrongs, but saying, in effect, "What we did was not wrong."

Who in the world says theft is not wrong? And yet, the monarchs of England blatantly flaunt their theft to the world at the highest political moment in their country—the coronation of their next queen.

In a context of world history, a demand to have a diamond returned to its rightful country must seem almost trivial. But in the first place, what nation would not rightly ask that its national treasures be returned? Much more than this, though, while Great Britain can never return the even more infinitely precious lives of Afghan people it has killed, and continues to kill, to return the Koh-i-Noor diamond would be a symbolic gesture at the very least—an acknowledgement of past wrongs, and perhaps even a signal that future wrongs would be no longer committed.

The British government will fulfill their moral and legal obligation if they return the Koh-i-Noor diamond back to Afghanistan from whence it was stolen. Such an act would do more to help the people of Afghanistan then continuing to kill them. Surely there are no millions of dollars that can determine the Koh-i-Noor's price for truly it is priceless. Its return would be equally priceless.

Hopefully it is clear why I close with this story. The true path to global peace, or at least a tremendous reduction in the current hostility and violence, is less complicated than many people imagine. Instead of thousands upon thousands of soldiers, just one envoy bringing home the Koh-i-Noor diamond—just one person saying, "Very well, we will de-occupy the Al-Aqsa Mosque tomorrow"—would make a world of difference. Of course, this means having to acknowledge past wrongdoing, and to desist from the perpetuation of current wrongdoing. Human greed, as much as pride, makes this difficult, but once again, the world can learn from the example of the people of Afghanistan, who are quick to admit wrongdoing, who are ashamed not to.

The admission may be difficult, but it is the first step. A simple act, like returning the Koh-i-Noor diamond, symbolizes precisely such a step. It is my sincere hope that the governments of the Anglo-American-Israeli alliance show that they have the moral fortitude to do so.